RIDING AND JUMPING

RIDING AND JUMPING

by William Steinkraus

Doubleday & Company, Inc., Garden City, New York
1961

Library of Congress Catalog Card Number 60-15754
Copyright © 1961 by William Steinkraus
All Rights Reserved
Printed in the United States of America
First Edition

TO MY TEACHERS

TABLE OF CONTENTS

RIDING AND JUMPING

Riders and Readers

Riders and Readers

I have often wondered why riders seem to spend so little time reading about the techniques of their sport as compared to participants in such activities as, say, golf or skiing. Is it because of the oft-repeated remark that "you can't learn to ride by reading a book about it"? Whatever the reason, the result is unfortunate; for while I would not be so foolhardy as to deny that this statement *is* true in its way, surely "its way" depends heavily on what we mean by the word, "riding."

Riding is surely one of the most versatile of all sports—it offers so many different rewards to its proponents. While the horse has lost his importance as a form of transportation for most of us, in many areas of the world he remains the most practical means of getting from one place to another and he is still the best way to follow a pack of hounds. Many doctors prescribe riding as a therapeutically useful activity. Riding also provides varieties of kinesthetic pleasure for people ranging from the city-bred stenographer in Central Park to the sailor on shore-leave. Of course, as practiced by the great international riders, the Spanish Riding School of Vienna, and the Cadré Noir, riding approaches an art.

"You just face the head, and put one leg on each side." Well, yes, that's riding, and it's good advice—but this book is not addressed to the nonrider who would like details as to which leg on which side, or the exercise-seeker, or the nature-lover who communes most effectively from horse-back. I do not decry these activities, nor can I deny that they, too, are a part of riding. But the reader who may, I hope, find something of value in the comments that follow will be one who has already defined his riding objectives more explicitly. He (or she, of course) will be one who is not frightened by the thought of being a "serious rider," and who will be challenged by the idea of acquiring the skills that will enable him to excel in the hunting field or in the show ring. Such a reader will already have been initiated into some of the basic mysteries of the relationship between man and horse, and on his (or her) level there is much that can be found in print that will facilitate the achievement of his goal.

When does a person start to ride? In one sense, the first time he puts "one leg on each side." But in the sense in which riding is meaningful to me, the rider starts to ride when he begins to contemplate the how's and why's as well as the what's of riding, and begins to concern himself with the education and improvement of his horse. (The distinction between "what" and "how" almost disappears on the more sophisticated levels of riding, for the most difficult things can hardly be done at all except in a certain way.)

I do not think there is a great deal to be gained by commencing the "one leg on each side" phase of riding at too early an age. Below the age of nine or ten, the child is unlikely to have either the strength, the size, or the coordination to do very many things correctly. He can develop his sense of balance, and gain confidence; but confidence is also sometimes irretrievably lost at this stage. For every rider I can think of who appears to have benefited from starting at a *very* early age, I can think of another who no longer rides at all, or almost forces himself to do so.

In my own case, I started when I was nine, and did relatively little riding until I was eleven. I can remember envying contemporaries of mine who had started at seven and seemed unapproachably far ahead of me at ten; but within a year or two, the gap had vanished. Neither of my parents was a rider, and it always seemed to me as a child that my strange passion for horses was more tolerated than encouraged—in any case, I never seemed able to do as much riding as I would have liked. Quite possibly there was much more encouragement from my parents than I realized at the time, but I am grateful to them for not having permitted me to become too early satiated with riding, or to regard riding as more of an obligation than a treat. So many children of fine horsemen, who get every encouragement from their parents to follow in their footsteps, lose their enthusiasm for riding very early because the riding is so *available*, and so easily becomes a matter of "If you don't exercise your pony today, you can't watch television before dinner."

But if the first step in riding is often taken too early, it seems to me that the next step—that of thinking about it as a meaningful activity, an exercise for the mind as well as the body, a process of mutual, reciprocal education of both horse and rider—often comes too late. Because of the widespread preconception that you can only learn, in a sort of intuitive way, by doing, and that reading or even thinking seriously about riding is rather pointless, too many young riders are doomed to groping too long in a forest of problems solved long ago.

I can recall my astonishment, when I first began to collect books on the techniques of riding, at finding, in books written two or three *centuries* ago, minute descriptions of "discoveries" that I had made for myself only after a long period of trial and error. I can recall it easily because I am still interested in reading about riding, and the same thing continues to happen regularly—so regularly, in fact, that I wonder if we don't truly understand only those things which we have already verified for ourselves. Most likely this is more apparent than true, for I am sure that my own development as a rider could have been very much accelerated if I could have been introduced at a very much earlier age to some of the thoughts and attitudes and basic concepts that are contained in the classic literature of riding.

Once we become interested in learning about riding, and are not content to repeat interminably the same errors, there is much that we can learn. The advice we receive directly from our riding masters is important, of course, but we must learn, too, from our own experimentation, from the careful observation and analysis of good riders, and espe-

cially from our horses—from their response to our efforts to
find a better way. We must constantly look for common
denominators in all these areas, for in each of them we
will find the same basic principles expressed in a variety
of different forms.

No two people sharing the same experience will respond
to it in exactly the same way, nor will they express their
reactions to it alike. That is why I hope that the present
selection of ideas and observations may prove helpful to
somebody else. I am not prepared to set forth a definitive,
comprehensive "system" of riding on the order of recent
valuable works by Seunig[1] or d'Endrödy[2]; I am still
learning from them (I hope!), and see no reason to restate
or reiterate the things they have already so explicitly expressed. But if there is a reason why people who read
such excellent books do not always turn into very much
better riders by the time they arrive at "Finis," it is
probably because it is difficult to maintain a clarity of
emphasis or focus in a work that is so comprehensive in
detail. The forests are lost in the trees.

In any case, I have found it very useful (and for that
matter, almost unavoidable) to supplement my reading
with conversations and exchanges of opinion on riding
problems with my fellow competitors, and I am still always
interested to learn what any successful rider regards as
especially significant factors in the art of riding. I have
found that there are two sides to learning from somebody
who is currently subjecting his theories to the acid test of

---

[1] *Horsemanship* by Waldemar Seunig, Doubleday, 1956.
[2] *Give Your Horse a Chance* by A. L. d'Endrödy, Allen,
1959.

competition: on the one hand, you may be sure that his ideas bear some relation to current practices; but on the other, his preoccupation with specific problems of the moment rather than broader generalities may easily cause a different kind of loss of perspective, and not only do the trees often stand out too prominently in word as in print, they sometimes seem to change their foliage seasonally as the problems of the moment change!

I mention these reservations about conversations on riding mainly because the pages that follow will consist of something more like a series of conversational observations on riding problems than the exposition of a complete "system" of riding. If it seems like a rather one-sided conversation—well, I'm afraid that friends who are familiar with some of my monologues on riding matters will say it's only characteristic.

CHAPTER 2

The Rider's Wherewithal

The Rider's Wherewithal

Wherewithal, that is, aside from money. Clothes don't make the rider, and I don't mean to imply that some particular kind or quality of clothing, or tack, or even horse is essential to the kind of "meaningful" riding that was discussed in Chapter 1. (Indeed, the contrary would be truer, for one can learn something from almost every riding experience.) But *some* kind of tack and horse and rider's equipment is a prerequisite, and there are vast differences among them. So before we start riding, let us consider briefly what sort of animal we will be riding, and what we will be riding him with.

First of all, horses are like people. Not too literally, of course, but in the sense that the horse population contains a virtually infinite range of individuals, individual in temperament, in physical structure, and in past experience. As a group, they are probably more generous, more forgiving, and less neurotic than people; but they are all different, and all living. This means that our relationship with each of them will be different from our relationship with every other, and that it will be a dynamic relationship, subtly or perhaps not so subtly changing every day. We can draw many broad generalizations about horses, just as we can about people; but we must be grateful rather than annoyed when something that "works" with one horse doesn't work with another, for it is this infinite and dynamic range of individual variation that makes riding a sport that can sustain our interest for a lifetime.

Within this vast range of individual variation, what qualities should we especially cherish? As with people, in the final analysis the temperamental qualities are more important than the physical ones. Since the rider's goal is to make the most of his horse, honesty, generosity, and a reasonably healthy stability of temperament will do much to simplify his task. Congenital rogues are happily rather rare in the horse population, though they do exist, especially in certain blood lines. Sometimes the rogue is possessed of so much ability that he is worth working with despite the temperamental deficiency; but on the average, a really defective temperament will lead to more frustration and disappointment than the effort is worth, and should be avoided. (I should make clear that by "congenital rogue" I do not mean simply the spoiled horse, the high-strung horse, or the horse who is frightened because of past abuse; I mean the horse who is fundamentally dishonest in the sense that he will try to cheat you any time the opportunity presents itself, and not only when provocation exists.)

Spoiled horses, difficult horses, and even rogues can teach us much that is important; the rider who is too well mounted may never really learn to ride. In this sense, the rider should not be too quick to avoid getting on the kind of horse he fears "will make him look bad," or the kind of horse that is especially difficult for him to ride. No horse is perfect, and often the skills acquired in working unsuccessfully with the very difficult problem horse will be sufficient to produce success with one only slightly less difficult.

The first horse I ever owned was, I suppose, a disappointment, for he never acted like a "child's horse" from the day he left the dealer's yard. He was "hot" just barely this side of being dangerous, and I won few ribbons with him; but I learned from him means of dealing with the excitable horse that enabled me for a long time to deal with that problem more successfully than any other. Later on, I had to force myself quite consciously to spend some time working with placid, sluggish horses—a side of my education which this first purchase had quite neglected.

The survey of leading horses of almost any year will point up the paradoxical relationship between temperament and physique. Few people would buy a Pegasus, an Earlsrath Rambler, or a Trader Bedford as great jumpers on the strength of their conformation alone. And we have all seen the horse who, to see him standing still, *should* jump six feet without turning a hair, but who can hardly jump three feet twice in succession without a wreck. Nonetheless, other things being equal, the horse with a better physical structure (very often the thoroughbred, who has been bred as an athlete) is more worth working with because we may make relatively less of his physical gifts and still achieve the same result.

Ideally, form and function are so closely related in horses that the most beautiful mechanism will also be the soundest mechanism. But it is a common failing to admire a beautiful head, a lovely topline, or even an attractive color so much that we neglect to really scrutinize the foot and the leg and the way of moving that much more truly "make" the horse. Every rider should learn as much about soundness as he can, for all of his skills as a rider will be of no avail if he is to put his best efforts into actual or potential cripples.

The temperamental qualities one looks for are easier to generalize about than the physical; I can think of a number of successful horses who conspicuously lack some, or even most, of the physical characteristics I prefer to see in a jumper. Some ewe-necked or short-fronted horses make excellent jumpers—for example, Nautical and Pegasus. But a good length of front, set on the right way, simplifies many problems. Long-backed horses like Hollandia and Ksar d'Esprit often have enormous ability and a special ease in jumping big spread fences, but most of them are hard to "hold together"; they tend to "come in installments" and flatten out over their fences. Shorter-backed horses like Halla, Merano, and Riviera Wonder tend to be able to do more things well, and are closer to my ideal pattern for a jumper.

Generally speaking, the good big horse will be able to do more than the good little horse, especially in jumping, but here too, it is dangerous to generalize too broadly. Little Squire, who was only 13.2 hands high, beat all the best horses of his era before the war with surprising regularity; Bambi, silver medalist in the 1952 Olympic Games at Helsinki under Oscar Cristi, could hardly have made fifteen hands; and Hugh Wiley's famous Nautical must stand on tiptoes to make sixteen hands. Nonetheless, for every little horse that "rides big" there are dozens of little horses that must really struggle to carry 165 pounds—the minimum weight for men under international rules—around the course. All other things equal, I would prefer a horse to be in the range of 16.1 to 17.0 hands high. Beyond seventeen hands we begin to find a diminishing return; very large horses tend to be rather clumsy, and are prone to unsoundness and respiratory problems. Geldings are quite widely preferred to mares, principally because they are more likely to have the right size and temperament. (And there is always the threat that a mare may come into heat just before an especially important competition.) However, mares tend perhaps to be more sensitive, and if this quality is utilized intelligently it can be an enormous asset. (Witness the relationship between Hans Winkler and Halla, whose consistency in the most important competitions over a period of years is a challenge to all the prejudices against the equine fair sex.)

In terms of movement, the best jumpers frequently show a higher action, or an action with more knee in it, than would be ideal in a show hunter. And there is almost a tradition of good jumpers who stood a bit too far over at the knee—Halla is again a case in point. The most important qualities to look for in the horse's movement are good natural balance, natural impulsion, and freedom from serious interference. It is often helpful to observe the basic way of moving as well as the basic jumping mechanism in a loose school, or on a longe line, for horses that have been badly spoiled frequently present a very false picture of themselves under tack.

Even over small fences in a corral one's attention should be focused on the way the horse bends his knees and rounds his back. The best jumpers seem to know how to do these things almost through instinct, and the horse who just naturally "snaps his knees" is on his way to a correct (and safe) jumping mechanism. There is always the exception, of course. Velvet Lassie was such a phenomenally good jumper that she never really learned to bend her knees, but just jumped that much higher; and that other outstanding mare, Pabst Brew, used to tuck her legs up too much under the belly; but on average, we should prize the instinct to bend the knees and round the back almost above everything else in the jumper. "Almost," because there is yet one more precious quality—the desire to jump fences clean. We can't expect the green horse not to make mistakes, but the horse we want will try harder the next time. It is all right if he still tries in the wrong way, for we can correct that—but nothing is more frustrating than the horse who will hit a fence hard, and come right back and hit it again from not caring rather than from not knowing how.

The rider's first mounted trial of a horse should be genuinely exploratory—an effort to find out as much about him as possible. It is quite a common tendency, in trying horses, to try to prove to the dealer or those who are watching how well one rides by carefully avoiding any area of difficulty that is exposed or even suspected. But in the long run, we will have to live with the reality and not with the appearance, and problems may just as well be explored a bit at the beginning as later on, when we start to work on them. (I don't mean to suggest that a full-scale attack on all of the horse's physical and psychological problems should be launched any time a friend or a dealer puts you up on something new; but one is hardly much wiser when he gets off a horse who has not been asked to stop, or turn, or even to really accept the rider's weight or leg while he was on his back.)

Saddlery

Just as some camera "bugs" are constantly exchanging cameras with the idea that somehow the picture is in the camera and not in their own skill, the rider who apparently hopes to find a certain "right" saddle that will automatically "make" his seat for him is a familiar figure. Unfortunately, good saddles can't help you as much in a positive way as bad saddles can annoy you and make it more difficult for you to sit well. But the good rider will ride well even on a bad saddle, while the best saddle can do nothing to help the poor rider. In principle, I think genuine learning is facilitated most by saddles that have the fewest protuberances and extra panels and extra rolls; but once the basic skills of sitting on a horse have been acquired, the choice of saddles becomes largely a personal matter dictated by the individual rider's particular physical structure. That the lowest point of the saddle should be directly in the center, and not three quarters of the way back, is not, I think, a matter of taste, and I think that most riders benefit from a relatively narrow tree and not too much bulk directly under the leg. But, beyond that, each may suit himself.

One never expects to spend much time losing stirrup irons and when one prefers rather lighter tack than the average, as I do, one is tempted to be consistent about the stirrup irons too. However, a reasonably wide and reasonably heavy iron will be far more easily recovered in emergencies—and this is exactly when a second or two saved may prove quite crucial in the show ring.

In regard to bridles, I doubt that quite so much weight and thickness as is commonly seen is really necessary. When only a snaffle bit is being used, reins with rubber hand parts are probably the most practical, but it is worth the trouble to find or order a pair made on a ⅝-inch or ¾-inch rein, and one that has longer hand parts than the standard American 1-inch racing rein. With a full bridle or Pelham, I find ⅝-inch x ¾-inch reins quite large enough —but this may be because I have relatively small hands, and the thicker reins seem to hinder both strength and sensitivity for me. Drop nosebands have been very much the fashion for jumpers ever since the War, and I generally use them too. I've never found them to be any miraculous panacea for bad mouths, but I think they do tend to inhibit such evasions as putting the tongue over the bit, which can be a very difficult habit to break once it's started.

I use running martingales almost as a general practice, always adjusting them so that there is no action on the rein at all when the horse's head is normally placed; so employed, they function only during the "awkward moment," and are not used to gain a mechanical advantage that will enable the rider to *pull* the horse's head in place. I suppose that the standing martingale can be adjusted to perform the same function, but in practice it seems to me that horses tend to lean against it if it is short enough to have any real effect at all. Draw reins can be very helpful when used with expert discretion, but are easily abused by the less skillful rider. (General J. T. Cole's oft-used phrase for this is extremely apt: "The razor in the monkey's hand.")

"Gimmicks," patent bits, and various combinations of martingales and draw reins will never be a substitute for hands—or more particularly, for the combination of hands and seat that is really the "mouth-making" mechanism. They may, under special circumstances, prove to be satisfactory temporary expedients, but at best, they should never be regarded as permanent solutions. It has often been said that the only real solution to any bitting problem will be based upon the use of the snaffle bit, and I believe this to be true. However, it is obvious that it is possible for a horse to have something less than a perfect mouth and still show with conspicuous success. When this is so, there is no reason why the horse should not continue to compete, in whatever bit he goes best in—but the normal work of improving his mouth at home should continue in a snaffle bridle, lest the rider find that his favorite "temporary expedient" is losing its effectiveness and must be constantly changed.

The Rider's Clothing

Clothes don't make a rider any more than saddles do, and yet curiously enough, good riders always somehow look the part, even on the ground. In the long run, the best quality is probably the best economy. Ready-made boots

and breeches are more practical, of course, for the young
rider who is growing rapidly; but the older rider is probably
better advised to have his boots and breeches made, and
to take all the time and trouble necessary to get the
neatest fit his maker can achieve. I have never been able
to feel that I was riding well in clothes that fit poorly, and
breeches that are loose at the knees have always been a
particular aggravation of mine. Such breeches are likely to
be very hard on the skin of the knees if used for jumping;
if they *must* be used, it is a wise precaution to protect the
danger area in advance with a patch of adhesive elastic
bandage.

Riding with or without gloves is a matter of personal
taste, but I think that more of the best riders wear gloves
than do without them. I used to really hate to wear
gloves, and suffered the inconvenience of occasionally tear-
ing patches of skin from between my fingers in hot weather.
Having now become accustomed to riding with gloves,
I find that the loss of "feel" is negligible, while the tacki-
ness of the leather seems to provide a better purchase on
the reins at the same expenditure of strength.

Finally, there is the matter of whips and spurs. Once a
rider has gained complete control of his leg position—
and only then—he should wear spurs, but at that point he
may as well make a standard practice of wearing them.
Spurs broaden the range of indications a rider can give his
horse with the leg, and the sensitive end of this range is
even more important than the severe end. Many authorities
decry the use of sharp spurs at any time, but dull rowels do
prove useful, worn only occasionally, for the horse who
has started to take the leg and the dull spur too much

for granted. Even in this case, of course, they must be used with very great control and judgment.

The whip should be neither too stiff nor too limber, and so balanced that it fits nicely in the hand. I think it is a sound policy to never get on a horse without a stick. One never knows when it will be needed, and when it is, the moment for correct application passes much too quickly to afford an opportunity to get off and get one. Even though a horse "doesn't need a stick" he should accept its presence with equanimity. The rider will find it an advantage to alternate occasionally the hand with which he carries the stick; sometimes just carrying it in the left hand will be enough to discourage the horse who has acquired the habit of always attempting his disobedience to the left, because he knows the stick is always carried in the right hand.

Once your horse is tacked up, don't complain about the shortcomings of bad equipment preventing you from achieving the results you should—if something is wrong, change it! Every *really* good rider I know takes considerable pains in the selection and care of the essential tools of his trade; there are no "bonus points" awarded for *almost* succeeding despite wretched equipment, and it is not that difficult to get everything right.

CHAPTER 3

Riding Basics I

PRELIMINARY CONSIDERATIONS AND POSITION

Riding Basics I

PRELIMINARY CONSIDERATIONS AND POSITION

In riding as in other activities it is a truism—though a commonly violated one—that you have to walk before you can run. Before you do either, of course, you have to get on your horse. It is surprising how clumsily this is done by many experienced riders, and few of us have really trained our horses to stand while we mount. The "leg up" from a groom and his restraining hand on the horse's bridle are fine for the short of stature, the elderly, and the unfit. But the rest of us should make it a practice always to mount from the ground. True, it may not often be necessary to mount without assistance; but when it is necessary, following a fall in the hunting field or the show ring, for example, skill in mounting from the ground is apt to be a real convenience at the very least, and under some circumstances it may quite literally "save the day."

No matter how you get on, there should be at least one invariable preliminary to mounting: checking the girth. If a groom has led the horse out for you, it is wise to run an eye over all the tack to ensure that the bit is placed properly in the horse's mouth, that the martingale is the right length, and that all keepers are tucked in. For those who have tacked up the horse themselves, this should not be necessary; but in any case, check the girth again, for just the short walk out of the barn will often give you a hole or two more slack (or even more, in the case of the horse that "blows up" when being girthed).

Once the rider has verified that the girth is sufficiently firm, he should adjust both reins so that they are even, and grasp the horse's withers with his left hand, facing at right angles to the horse (or if necessary, *slightly* toward the rear) while his right hand adjusts the stirrup iron on the *toe* of his left foot. (Any reasonably sensitive horse has a right to take exception to the rider who puts his foot all the way "home" in the stirrup, and gives him a sharp jab in the ribs as the toe turns forward.)

At this point, my practice deviates slightly from the orthodox, for I prefer not to grasp the cantle with the right hand, but to reach *across* the seat of the saddle instead and grasp its far edge just behind the juncture of the skirt. While this will be quite a long reach for the rider who is of short or medium height, or when the horse is exceptionally tall, the rider will find his grasp much more secure—and this can be a great advantage when one is attempting to mount really "green" or "rough" horses. Once the purchase on the far side of the saddle has been gained, the actual act of mounting is facilitated, and even more important, the tendency of the saddle to turn on the horse's back is minimized.

Two final points about mounting. The simplest way of dealing with the horse who moves away from the rider as he starts to mount is to shorten the outside rein, so that the horse's body must turn toward, rather than away from the rider if the horse takes a step. And once "on top," the rider should take pains to settle *very* gently into the saddle; the horse must not start the day's riding with the idea already established in his mind that he must somehow protect himself from the rider's weight.

Once mounted, the rider's first act should be to put himself and his horse in order. More particularly, he immediately establishes two balances: the horse's, by asking him to stand evenly on all four legs; and his own, by distributing his weight evenly in the exact center of the saddle. In other words, he must at the same time ask his horse to carry him, and make himself fit to be carried. If this is done correctly both centers of gravity will feel as if they are in the same vertical line.

Not only is it true that we must walk before we run, but we must learn to stand before we can walk. A slipshod, or careless, or incorrect beginning is a poor foundation for the time to be spent on horseback, and if I seem overly insistent on this point, it is only that the fault of moving out at a walk before anything is in the right place or in the right balance is so extremely common.

POSITION

The elements of the rider's position have already been discussed so clearly, and in such minute detail, by such writers as Müseler,[1] d'Endrödy, and Seunig, that there seems no need to elaborately duplicate their efforts here. These modern classics of riding should be in the library of every serious horseman, and the precepts they contain should be studied and restudied until the rider is thoroughly familiar with them. Position is only a means to an end, and not an end in itself—but it is so essential a means that the rider must reconcile himself to checking and rechecking his position all his riding life.

When I first became interested in books on riding (long before the above-mentioned works had become available), I happened to acquire *The History and Art of Riding* by Richard Berenger (London, 1771). Berenger, who was Gentleman of the Horse to George III, stated the basic elements of position in a way that seemed quite lucid to me at that time, and on rereading him, his emphases still seem well placed. (To be fair, most of the credit should go to the French writer Bourgelat, from whom Berenger's ideas are largely drawn.) Perhaps the reader will find, as I did, that this voice from an earlier age is both quaintly amusing and instructive in what it says about the subject at hand:

In order to succeed in an art where the mechanism of the body is absolutely necessary, and where each

[1] *Riding Logic* by W. Müseler, Scribner's, 1937.

part of the body has its proper functions, which are
peculiar to that part, it is most certain that all and
every part of the body should be in a natural posture.
Were they in an imperfect situation, they would want
that ease and freedom which is inseparable from grace;
and as every motion which is constrained being false in
itself, and incapable of justness, it is clear that the part
so constrained and forced would throw the whole into
disorder, because each part belonging to and depending upon the whole body, and the body partaking of
the constraint of its parts, can never feel that fixed
point, that just counterpoise and equality, in which
alone a fine and just execution consists. . . .

Let the horseman place himself at once upon his twist
(fork) sitting exactly in the middle of the saddle; let
him support this posture in which the twist alone
seems to sustain the weight of the whole body, by
moderately leaning upon his buttock; let his thighs be
turned inward and rest flat on the sides of the saddle;
and, in order to do this, let the turn of the thighs proceed directly from the hip, and let him employ no
force or strength to keep himself in the saddle, but
trust to the weight of his body and thighs; this is the
exact equilibre; in this consists the firmness of the
whole building, a firmness which young beginners are
never sensible of at first, but which is to be acquired
and will always be attained by exercise and practice. . . .

The head should be free, firm, and easy, in order to be
ready for all the natural motions that the horseman
may make in turning to one side or the other. It should
be firm, that is to say, straight, without leaning to the
right or left, neither advanced nor thrown back; it
should be easy, because if otherwise, it would occasion

a stiffness, and that stiffness affecting the different parts
of the body, especially the backbone, they would be
without ease, and constrained.

The shoulders alone influence by their motion that
of the breast, the reins (loins), and the waist.

The horseman should present or advance his breast; by
that his whole figure opens and displays itself; he should
have a small hollow in his reins, and push his waist
forward to the pommel of the saddle, because this
position corresponds and unites him to all the motions
of the horse. Now only throwing the shoulders back,
produces all these effects, and gives them exactly in
the degree that is requisite; whereas, if we were to look
for the particular position of each part separately, and
by itself, without examining the connection that there
is between the motions of one part with those of
another, there would be such a bending in his loins,
that the horseman would be, if I may so say, hollow
backed; and as from that he would force his breast
forward, and his waist toward the pommel of the
saddle, he would be flung back, and must sit upon the
rump of the horse. . . .

The legs should be kept near the sides of the horse,
and in a line with the man's body; for being near the
part of the horse's body where his feeling is most
delicate, they are ready to do their office in the instant
they are wanted. Moreover, as they are an appendix of
the thighs, if the thigh is upon its flat in the saddle,
they will by a necessary consequence be turned just
as they ought, and will infallibly give the same turn
to the feet, because the feet depend upon them as they
depend upon the thighs.

The toe should be held a little higher than the heel . . . Many persons, notwithstanding, when they raise their toe, bend and twist their ankle as if they were lame in that part. The reason of this is very plain: It is because they make use of the muscles in their legs and thighs, whereas they should employ only the joint of the foot for this purpose; a joint given by nature to facilitate all the motions of the foot, and to enable it to turn to the right or left, upwards or downwards . . . Such is, in short, the mechanical disposition of all the parts of the horseman's body. I will enlarge no farther on subjects treated already so amply by every writer; it is needless to write what has already been handled.

Berenger's emphasis on weight as a substitute for strength, on ease, and on equilibrium is very sound. In horsemanship classes one quite often sees a seat which is apparently correct, but which is maintained by strength rather than by balance, and thus creates an impression that it is painful for the rider to maintain it. Effort defeats its own purpose, for the forced seat cannot be a really successful means for anything. It is a happy circumstance, and no accident, that the right way in anything involving a physical mechanism is also the easiest way. And it is sad that some of the most conscientious students are frustrated in their ambitions by a willingness to translate their conscientiousness into sustained effort.

Sustained effort must exist in riding, but it should be the sustained effort of finding the right way, of making the correct—and easy—application of the principles being studied. The effort that is necessary to maintain an incorrect position and to force the muscles into reproducing correct symptoms without having been able to establish correct causes for those symptoms, may be an admirable exercise of will power, or a revealing indication of the rider's ability to support discomfort. But I very much doubt whether such efforts will be rewarded by success.

It is true of the horse, too, that little can be achieved by constant forcing. It is relatively rare that the resistance we encounter in schooling derives from a genuine obstinacy of temperament; more often what we would like the horse to do is quite obvious, even to him, but we have failed to show him any comfortable way to do it. (I presume that what is demanded of the horse will not often be really impossible for him, but the way in which we ask for it or the time at which we ask may *make* it impossible.)

Let us presume, for example, that the rider is sitting correctly, and has put his horse to the aids, "according to the book" as he understands it. He may do almost everything right, but if he forgets that the horse can only answer his aid with the leg that is *about to leave the ground*, he will never make it possible for the horse to obey him promptly and he will probably regard this failure as resistance.

Continued resistance in the horse, and continued frustrations of the rider's best intentions, far more often indicates that something is being done wrong than it reflects the horse's stubbornness or the rider's lack of perseverance or "talent." When such resistance in the horse, or lack of co-ordination in the rider, is encountered, the rider's first reaction should *not* be merely to repeat the error; he must try to discover the error in what he is doing, which is to say, find a better way.

I am afraid that stubbornly repeating errors must have been a natural inclination of mine, because I can well remember "Cappy" Smith telling me, on more than one occasion, "If you try something often enough, and it doesn't even start to work, for heaven's sake, try something else." This is very pragmatic advice, and it is a principle that is very naturally applied by the kind of good rider who has never tried to learn about riding from reading books. (I suspect that this explains the curious pair of horseshow opposites: the person who is a gifted rider on a verbal level, and sometimes quite sound in what he says, but who cannot really ride a horse at all; and the person who gets good results on horseback without being able to find much relationship between the "experts'" theories and his own experiences. The former is probably misapplying principles which are in themselves sound. The latter cannot do this, for he doesn't know enough theories to be able to misapply them; he has simply rejected things that "didn't work" until he found things that did, and thus has been able to develop a sound practice on no other theoretical basis than that "it works.")

If you are fortunate enough to work in an indoor ring that has a mirror, it can be a great help in learning to form a correct and comfortable position. (Don't be self-conscious about watching yourself; you are likely to hear some jokes about your vanity, and so do the riders of Olympic caliber, but they go right ahead and use the aid of a mirror, or even their reflection from a window whenever they can.) After a while you will find that if your balance and coordination with the horse are working properly, you can adapt yourself quite easily to many minor variations of position. And thus, if you can't achieve the position your teacher wants to see, the chances are that you are doing some quite basic thing wrong. The time to make your own adaptations of position comes when you can duplicate

your instructor's or anyone else's idea of the perfect seat,
and not before. As a matter of fact, it is a sound principle
never to discard the commonly accepted, "inferior" way of
working with horses for your own "superior" methods until
you are quite certain that you are applying the "old" techniques properly.

Most of the hard-bitten professional horsemen of my
acquaintance would maintain that the only real school for
riders is the "school of hard knocks." They are likely to
speak glowingly of the falls they took in their youth, and
the bad horses they rode, and maintain that this is the
only way to learn. They have a point, and I would agree
with them that in fact a considerable number of good
riders developed in this way. But the explanation is simply
that the person who is dealing with dangerous horses, or
the young professional with a barn full of mediocre horses
to sell, cannot enjoy the luxury of persisting for very long
in tactics that don't work. The techniques of riding, as I
have said, are means rather than ends; the end is the horse's
improvement.

What most of the graduates of the "schools of hard
knocks" have had to acquire for their diploma is a series of
expedient techniques that are often described as "crude but
effective." Such techniques are surely better than those
that are crude but ineffective, or those (which many of
the best-intentioned amateurs possess) not crude but not
effective either. However, it should be pointed out that the
most truly *effective* techniques are those which are not
crude at all; the connotations of the word "crude" suggest
a certain waste motion, and a "lesser of two evils" solution
of problems. The great riding techniques of our day, which
we can witness in the performances of a Winkler, a d'Inzeo,

a Chammartin, or a St. Cyr, need no apologetic "buts" at all; they are the techniques that in subtlety as well as effectiveness enable him to exploit, in the best sense of the word, all the potentialities of his horse.

CHAPTER 4

Riding Basics II

UNDERSTANDING THE HORSE'S MOVEMENT

Riding Basics II

UNDERSTANDING THE HORSE'S MOVEMENT

Although riding masters spend most of their teaching time
correcting details of position, and even experienced riders
find it necessary to keep their own position under constant
scrutiny, the real importance of position is as a means
rather than as an end. Correct position facilitates correct
function, and only correct functioning by the rider can
produce the correct movements of the horse by which our
ultimate riding goals are expressed. In other words, all our
most effective means of initiating and controlling the
horse's movement depend on a sound position; and it is
only by utilizing these means that we can get our horse to
move properly, and in turn carry us properly so that our
correct position can be effortlessly maintained.

If the horse's defenses—say, a stiff back and rough gaits—
can force us to compromise the soundness of our position,

then we will have permitted him to rob us of our only
means of penetrating those defenses.

It will be apparent that there is a similar relationship between position and function for the horse himself—the
movement we require from him may be made easy, difficult,
or even impossible according to the position from which
we ask him to execute it. (Even the most natural jumper
will hardly be able to round his back in jumping if his head
is "in your lap" as he leaves the ground.)

Since controlling the horse's movement is our major
concern, it is essential that we understand *how* the horse
moves—not necessarily in a detailed anatomical sense
(though such knowledge is worth gaining because it leads
to a clearer understanding of soundness), but in broad out-
line. A lot can be learned from studying the movement
of horses from the ground; it is often useful to be able to
translate the sensation of the horse's movement into the
visual picture of his movement and vice versa. But whether
we study the horse's actual anatomical structure, or watch
him from the ground, or feel him from his back, one
lesson should be clear, and it should never be forgotten;
the horse's motive power comes from the hind legs, or, to
put it another way, the horse is a rear-engined animal.
A moment's contemplation of the difference in size of the
bony and muscular structures of the hind legs as compared
to the front legs and their relative states of flexion immediately suggests that there is a sound basis for the old
adage about horses getting their hind legs under them, or
"jumping off their hocks." While it may be oversimplifying
to say that if you control the hind legs you control the horse,
it is much nearer to the whole truth than many riders
suspect.

The fact that only the evasions and resistances that occur in front of the saddle are visible to the rider is probably responsible for the prominence of "good hands" in the rider's thoughts and in the literature on riding. In fact, the "good hands" of a good rider will have relatively little to do; a very large part of the evasions and resistances that are visible in front of the saddle are only symptoms of evasions and resistances that originate in the hind legs, and the good rider will have the hind legs under control. The rider's legs and seat alone can initiate movement, and they also play the major role in controlling its direction, its intensity or impulsion, and its cadence. Hence the great importance of the sitting trot—as opposed to the posting trot—in schooling horses. The rider's seat bones can hardly influence the horse when they are not in contact with the horse's back, and the sitting trot enables the rider to employ their influence constantly instead of intermittently. The hands merely regulate the movements that have been initiated "from behind," and if the rider's movement-creating mechanism is working smoothly, they should have relatively few excesses to deal with.

Thus it will be seen that the phrases "to drive a horse up to the bit" and "to pull a horse together" are not really interchangeable at all. In fact the second phrase, still so commonly heard, can accomplish nothing but the opposite result if put into practice in the way that is implied—by pulling. The idea that we "pull a horse up" is just as common, just as apparently reasonable, and unfortunately just as unsound. Only the horse who is willing to go forward can make a correct halt. It is important for the rider to *always* feel that his horse is ready to move forward—even while he is backing—and this will never be possible when he has the sensation of supporting more of the horse with his hands than he is supporting with his seat and legs.

The idea that the horse picks up speed against the rider's will because he won't accept the rider's leg or because the rider can't make him "go forward" seems a contradiction in terms. (I must confess that I thought I was talking to a real eccentric the first time I encountered this concept.) Nonetheless, it is true; if you can really move the hind legs, you can stop the horse. More important, you can stop him correctly, which is to say in balance, and in a position that facilitates the next movement, whatever it may be.

Few horses will persevere in pulling against their riders when it involves a sustained expenditure of muscular strength to do so. Usually the "cold mouth" of the puller results from an altered distribution of weight rather than a sustained muscular effort: lazy hind legs refuse to reach far enough forward to maintain the horse's correct, natural balance, and force the rider to support the forehand with his hands. The farther forward the rider can get his horse to reach with his hind legs (or even better, to *swing*), the harder it will be for the horse to shirk the responsibility of carrying the rider's weight and maintaining his own balance by either boring against the bit, or raising his head and dropping behind it. Both of these defenses are facilitated by a hollow back, and the most convenient way for the horse to hollow his back is by slightly retarding the movement of the hind legs.

Thus the crucial moment in resistance usually comes when our "rear-engined" animal starts to lose "r.p.m." At this moment the rider's attention is drawn to the head, which is starting to come up, and the common instinct is to maintain contact by raising the hands. Unfortunately, the rider who follows this instinct will be concentrating on symptoms rather than causes; his real solution lies in re-establishing the liveliness of the hind legs, for he will never succeed in pulling the head back into place again, and the moment at which the hind legs start to move freely again is the only moment at which the head and neck can naturally reassume a correct carriage. One of the surest ways of preventing resistance from ever developing is to always ask of the horse just a little more movement than he offers, ensuring that the feeling of liveliness in the hind legs—of sufficient "r.p.m."—will be maintained.

It is an almost certain sign that you are not really moving the hind legs when you start to wish that you were just a little bit stronger. Since I do not have a particularly powerful build myself, I have more than once thought, "I'm just not strong enough to "come through" with this horse, and make him yield—but if I were just a bit stronger, I'd be able to." No! The rider is never strong enough to succeed through sheer brute strength.

I will never forget watching, one day in Germany, a rider working with one of the massive, cold-blooded Holstein horses. He was shirtless, and I could see his shoulders and biceps. He wasn't just a little stronger than I am, he must have been twice as strong—but strain as he might, he was getting nowhere with the horse he was riding. After a while a rather small, older man got on the horse, and started to drive the horse's hind legs under him and make him carry himself instead of leaning on the rider. As I watched him begin to succeed, and saw the horse's entire way of moving change, I really understood for the first time how little riding skill has to do with strength, and how doomed the rider is who enters into a pulling contest with a horse.

Surely this is implied in one of the most widely quoted of all riding axioms, Gustav Steinbrecht's "Ride your horse forward and hold it straight." Yet this trenchant advice of the great German horseman and writer is deceptive because it seems so simple, and so easy to put into practice; but those who have begun to really explore its richness of allusion will usually follow the quotation with "Yes, that is the difficult thing." By the time the serious rider has learned why this is true, he will also know what riding in its best sense is all about.

The "ride forward" part of the phrase above refers to the correct utilization of this rear-engined mechanism that we have already discussed. In the normal, well-balanced horse, it is the recovering of his natural balance, and natural freedom of movement. To be held straight, however, does not seem to be a natural condition for the horse, and one of his commonest defenses is simply crookedness—refusing to follow his head with a spinal column that is truly straight when working on straight lines, or *evenly* bent on turns. What we need in order to make a horse straight is an accurate and subtle corrective mechanism, and it is this end that is served by the various suppling and bending exercises. The horse's tendency toward deviation seems *always* to be there; and when we see a St. Cyr come down the center line of the dressage ring with every foot in the right place, it is not because the horse has learned to follow this line by himself, but because the incipient deviations have been corrected before they could actually take form.

Thus it is not enough to say that the rider's function is

merely one of eliciting the response he wants from the
horse in the correct way. He must also work constantly to
shape, correct, and refine the response he gets. This conception of the rider's function must, however, be tempered
by practical considerations. The horse cannot learn every
thing at once, and it is the number of correct responses the
rider gets, not the number of correct responses he asks for,
that really determines the rider's excellence. The right
thing, in the right way, and at the right time—it is the last
of these goals, the quality that is often referred to as
"equestrian tact," that is probably the most important.

In his daily work, as in his whole career, the horse's
number of correct responses will depend upon the adequacy
of his preparation. Things that may be eminently possible
in half an hour, or in a month, may be impossible now.
And if they cannot be done correctly, nothing will be
gained by forcing them to be done incorrectly. It is, of
course, quite possible to carry this precept so far that it
becomes ridiculous. The overmatched horse, who is faced
with difficult demands before he can consistently meet
simpler ones, is the commonest phenomenon, but the
perennial green horse, who is never quite ready to do anything, is also a familiar type.

The soundest practice is to make haste, and make the
most of our horses, neither slowly nor quickly, but *appro-*
priately, at the pace that is appropriate to the particular
horse we are riding. It is just as wrong to destroy the
freshness and the bloom of the gifted horse by repeating
endlessly exercises that he has already mastered as it is to
demand difficult movements from the horse who cannot
do the simple ones correctly. The judgment that enables us

to tell one from the other is something that we must work patiently to acquire. It will never be infallible, but it is an essential mark of the horseman, and will always distinguish him from those who merely ride well.

CHAPTER 5

Work on the Flat

Work on the Flat

If the reader identified himself with the rider who was told how to mount in Chapter 3, he has probably long since been wondering when the preliminaries will be finished so that he can get on with the business of riding. The time is now.

Having established our position, and asked the horse to stand on his four legs, we should begin our day's work in a pleasant, and even conciliatory way, establishing only a light contact at first, and asking the horse to accept our weight and leg in a very discreet way. It is important for the horse to enjoy his work, and not dread the rider's appearance on the scene as an inevitable preliminary to difficult and unreasonable demands and perhaps a fight. For the first few minutes, we should normally ask for nothing difficult, and require only easy things in a very natural, relaxed way.

It should not be necessary, however, to start every day with a long warming-up period on completely loose reins. This makes a nice treat for the horse the day after a hard school, or on days when only very light work is planned, but the horse must learn that he will not always have half an hour's indulgence before he is expected to start to think about what he is doing.

As soon as the edge of freshness begins to disappear and the horse starts to move freely and accept the rider's seat and leg, the demands may increase. With a strange horse, the rider will begin to explore his aptitudes and weaknesses, and his state of training. With a horse with whom we are already familiar, today's work will be dictated by yesterday's, although it may not necessarily start at the same place. The first demands are normally a little bending, and some halts and half-halts. Once these are in order on their simplest level, we may ask for them in more difficult forms, or proceed to work over *cavalletti*, or low fences, or figure eights, or whatever lies in the horse's training program. If these are not in order, and this will often be the case with the strange horse, we must correct the execution of these ABCs before attempting anything else.

As I have said, it is necessary to walk before you can run, and in fact, difficulties are usually best solved at the slower paces. If a horse's halts from a canter are faulty, the rider must be certain that they are correct from a trot, and if here, too, they are fallible, he must go back to walking until the halt is correctly performed at that pace.

I have often been asked about the desirability of dressage for the jumper. Since the French word *dressage* may be translated as "training," it is sometimes maintained that everybody practices dressage, in his own way, every second he is on horseback. This is not exactly true; for even aside from the specific context of the dressage arena, the word *dresser* tends to imply not only training but training according to rational principles. (Some of the secondary definitions of the word are "to straighten," "to level," and "to adjust"; the army command for straightening a line of troops, "Dress right," is an example of these meanings of the same basic word that has been preserved in English.)

In principle, there is no limit to the benefit that can be derived from the exercise of dressage movements for any horse, for their aim is to produce an animal who is supple, obedient, and balanced, objectives which are just as desirable in the hack as in the show horse. In practice, however, it must be admitted that certain dressage movements are almost like Pandora's box. Perfectly accomplished, they can be beneficial—but the skills that are necessary to accomplish them perfectly are rare, and possibly beyond the scope of the average rider. High collection, and such movements as the passage and piaffe that depend on it, have no explicit applications for the jumper, and, imperfectly attempted, they are likely to produce difficulties and resistances in the horse that quite outweigh the benefits that might be gained. The more advanced lateral movements, imperfectly achieved, may similarly be used as defenses by the horse.

What, then, are the real essentials for the jumper? Primarily, the rider must be able to control his horse's forward movement and impulsion in a smooth and evenly graduated way; he must be able to turn accurately and correctly; and it will be a great convenience if he can make a correct single flying change of lead. The turn on the haunches and on the forehand, the shoulder-in, and correct halts and half-halts are indispensable foundations for the achievement of these aims. The range of collection and extension that is really essential is, however, somewhat narrower than that required by the trained dressage horse. We must require from the jumper a high standard of excellence, relatively speaking, of the ordinary trot and the ordinary canter; but, on average, I think we should place more emphasis on extension than on collection.

Since both Seunig and d'Endrödy provide detailed, step-by-step programs for the horse's development, I will not deal more specifically with the particular contents of the day's program. I would like to emphasize, however, that judgment and discretion should always be in evidence in the rider's choice of the specific work he does. No program at all, or a haphazard one, is likely to produce slower progress than work that has a definite and progressive direction. However, the rider must guard equally against becoming too methodical by developing a daily work program that is rigid, unimaginative, and dull.

Older horses must quite frequently, in their show careers, perform extremely difficult acts with only a minimum of preparation, and sometimes they should practice this too. While normally a half-hour's work on the flat is the best preliminary for a "school," the older horses should occasionally be expected to jump with just a short warm-up as preliminary. I can remember Winkler, the former Olympic and World Champion, telling me that he felt this kind of variety was very beneficial in dealing with the difficult feminine temperament of Halla.

How long should the average day's work last, and how much should the rider attempt to do in a single day? A schedule that is based so much on the clock that the particular horse's response to the kinds of work being done is ignored defeats its own purpose. But on average, an hour's work a day should be enough, and the things that cannot be accomplished in an hour today should be left until tomorrow. There will always be exceptions, for it *is* sometimes necessary to "come through" with an especially difficult horse, and it is frustrating to stop the young horse's work just at the point when he seems on the verge of breaking through to a higher level of achievement; but the rider must avoid creating this kind of situation at the end of an hour *every* day by always finding an excuse to continue "a little longer." Sometimes the progress he imagines is really there, but more often the schooling sessions will simply get longer and longer until the horse that is being "hammered at" daily must be taken out of work altogether for reasons of soundness.

For light work, exercise when there is some physical reason for wishing to stay off the horse's back, or the early stages of remaking a very badly spoiled horse, the rider will find longeing an extremely useful way in which to accomplish part of his normal work on the flat. We don't see very much longeing in the United States, and what we do see is very often done so carelessly as to be dangerous physically and virtually useless educationally—the horse performing an oval rather than a circle around the rider, who occasionally throws a piece of loose dirt at him to keep him moving.

It is almost impossible to longe a horse properly without

the proper equipment—a longe line of sufficient length, a proper longeing whip, and side lines. (I find it more convenient to use the horse's normal saddle and bridle than the longeing cavesson and surcingle; the regular reins are slipped under the stirrups, which are tied up, and the longe line is passed through one ring of the bit, over the poll, and snapped or buckled to the ring on the other side.) But when longeing is properly performed, the good horseman can keep the horse between his hand and his whip almost as delicately as he could control him between his hand and leg in riding; and then the exercise can be equally beneficial, both in terms of the horse's state of condition and state of training.

Incidentally, one can never be too careful in starting the horse off on the circle when one is longeing, for a sudden release of the longe line and a cluck can leave the rider defenseless against the very fresh horse's instinct to wheel and kick. A very nice bay mare of mine ensured that I would remember this warning by breaking my arm with a kick one day when I was starting her off on the circle a trifle too casually.

When we first start to analyze all the factors that are involved in the interrelationship between the rider's movements and the horse's, it is easy to become overwhelmed by the complexity of even the simplest acts; there seem to be so many things to think about simultaneously that suddenly *everything* becomes difficult. One way of smoothing out the co-ordination of movement at such moments is to invent images that summarize and simplify the complex physical acts, substituting a single thing to concentrate on in place of many things.

Seunig's suggestion that the rider should feel his collar with the back of his neck is the sort of thing I have in mind. It is only one idea to think about, but the single image translates itself in practice into a change in the attitude of the entire upper body. I'm not sure that all these personal images work equally well for everyone, but I suspect that every rider can find ones that work—at least for him.

I have sometimes imagined, when riding sluggish horses who try to lean on my hands by always "holding back" with the hind legs, that their real intention is to "wheel": to suddenly stop, rear, and turn. If you have ever been thrown by a horse who has mastered this trick (as I have), you will find that a little self-deception in imagining this inclination in the sluggish horse will suddenly make you highly sensitive to the shortened steps with the hind legs that make wheeling possible. Automatically you will start to use your own legs, and refuse to establish the kind of dead hold with your hands that would compromise your safety on the wheeler.

Another very useful image was suggested to me by Bertalan de Nemethy, coach of our U. S. Olympic Team; he advises the rider to think of his reins as sticks, a conception which very effectively discourages the tendency to permit the outside shoulder of the horse to escape on turns, and encourages the rider to make the correction with his inside leg instead.

A word about voice aids. Even if I am only going to ride a horse for a short period of time, I always like to establish some kind of response to the voice aids of the "cluck" and the "whoa." The conditioned response involved can be very quickly established, by reinforcing the cluck with a quick, sharp tap of the whip a few times, and by reinforcing the whoa with some simultaneous full halts—and once established, it can function in all kinds of emergencies where nothing else can be done quite so promptly or delicately. I do not believe that the use of voice aids should become habitual, for then they tend to lose their effectiveness—not *every* full halt should be accompanied by a whoa, and not every sudden extension by a cluck. But they should be used often enough so that the horse maintains a fresh and clear understanding of their meanings, with all the range of inflection and intensity that can be used. Just a gentle "whoa, whoa" can be invaluable in steadying the nervous horse who sees the next fence and is tempted to make a break for it; and the cluck can revive impulsion in the horse who is starting to disregard the legs, without requiring the rider to take a hand off the reins as the use of the whip at that moment would do.

My last point in regard to normal work on the flat (and it applies equally to work over fences) is that the actual accomplishment of the day depends on the time spent dealing constructively with difficulties. To be sure, the horse's attitude of co-operation with the rider must always be encouraged and preserved. But one of the commonest of all failings is the tendency to practice primarily the thing one already does well, and casually, and sometimes even subconsciously, to avoid the areas of difficulty. It is fruitless to show off to friends and attempt to conceal problems during work—the show ring is the place for that. The good rider will often surprise you by how well his horse goes in the show ring compared to the schooling session you have watched. Far more frequently we see horses go less well in the ring. And surprisingly often we

will find that the problems revealed in the show ring
are scarcely touched in practice.

The show ring—or the formal school that duplicates the
conditions of the show ring—provides a useful check on our
areas of weakness. Once our problems have been redefined
under such circumstances, we must analyze them and
attempt to reduce them to their simplest forms so that we
can work on them at a level on which they are the same
in kind, but not in degree. In riding, it is the strength
of the foundation that determines the reliability of the
whole structure. Only by insisting that the simple things
are done well before making more difficult demands is
it possible to achieve a simultaneous development of the
rider's skills and his horse's abilities. The steady progress
that can be achieved in this way will make the day's work
a genuine pleasure for both.

CHAPTER 6

The Foundations for Jumping

The Foundations for Jumping

Most of the elements that make a good jump possible must be established during the approach, rather than during the act of jumping itself. Ideally, the jump itself is no more than the logical—or even inevitable—consequence of the preparation for it.

Since the success of the individual jump depends heavily on the quality of its approach, the level of the horse's jumping skill depends heavily upon the level of his basic training on the flat. Thus it will be seen that we have been talking about the preparation for jumping all along; the methods of schooling we will deal with now all demand, as a necessary prerequisite, a horse and rider whose basic skills are already firmly grounded.

A good jump depends upon the rider's ability to place the horse within the correct take-off area with the right impulsion, pace, and balance. The proportion of these three qualities may vary; pace may be moderate if impulsion is great, and even balance may be somewhat deficient if the combination of pace and impulsion is appropriate to the fence at hand. It follows that the rider's position and ability to influence his horse correctly during the approach is far more important than his position during the flight of the jump itself. Indeed, it is by no means uncommon to find successful riders whose position in the air may be described as anything from eccentric to thoroughly unsound; but I cannot think of a consistently successful rider whose position during the approach has not had much more orthodox virtues to recommend it. (To be sure, one may find fault with some of the extreme individualists during the approach as well, but such riders are usually limited to a relatively narrow range of horses that they can ride successfully.)

For example, the rider who has little use of his legs and seat will depend upon the amount of natural impulsion his horse happens to bring with him; for his only other means of creating impulsion—the whip and the cluck—are too crude to permit the kind of accuracy that is required in riding sound approaches. By the same token, the rider whose position only feels secure to him when his legs are "halfway through the horse" is likely to have little success with high-strung horses as a group. Ideally, the rider will have found the position that enables him to evoke the widest possible range of response from his horse with the minimum of effort and displacement of position on his part. Before he commences the business of jumping, such a rider will have developed the ability to preserve both his horse's physical and temperamental bal-

ONE OF MY FIRST SHOWS—TWEEDLEDUM AT FAIRFIELD IN 1937

This was my first pony, and he taught me a lot, as good ponies will. Not exactly a stellar show-ring performer (the out gate tended to exert a strong magnetic pull on him), he still sticks in my memory as quite a dashing performer in the hunting field and a rather obstinate but very forgiving friend. *Photo: I. Cantor.*

A COUPLE OF EXPERIMENTS FARTHER AFIELD

I couldn't make much pretense of really knowing how to set up a saddle horse, or of being a brilliant amateur whip, but I do think that we can learn something of value from all kinds of experience with all kinds of horses, and I very much enjoyed "fooling around" with polo and driving and race horses and saddle horses. The top picture was taken in 1942 at a War Bond carriage parade at Belmont Park, the bottom in 1940 when I used to ride in saddle-seat equitation classes. *Top Photo: I. Cantor. Bottom Photo: Carl Klein.*

CAPTAIN BERTALAN DE NEMETHY LONGEING
MISS ELEANORA SEARS'S KSAR D'ESPRIT

In this picture the coach of our Olympic Equestrian Team is helping Ksar to find his right balance on the longe line and to move forward freely with his head in place and his back muscles relaxed. On this occasion draw reins have replaced the more customary side lines, and instead of using a longeing caveson, Bert has simply run the longe line through the off ring of the snaffle bit and snapped it on the other side. There is nothing sloppy about the way Ksar is moving, and nothing sloppy about the way Bert is longeing him; the horse is just as delicately balanced between the hand and the longeing whip as he would be between Bert's hand and leg if he were riding.

STIRRUPS TIED UP FOR LONGEING

This close-up shows more clearly how the length of the draw rein can be adjusted by knotting and also reveals the most practical means of tying up stirrups: starting with the stirrup irons run up normally, the loop in the leathers is led first over the iron but underneath itself from behind, and then brought back under the iron but over itself. If the free end of the leather is then run through the small loop that remains, the position of the iron will be absolutely secure.

A TYPICAL GYMNASTIC EXERCISE

This three-combination consists of a relatively vertical fence with a good ground line and two square oxers, the first in a long distance, the second in a short one. Rustic materials such as these are excellent for schooling, for they encourage the green horse's confidence and enable him to concentrate his whole attention on the nature of the problem that has been presented. *Photo: Budd Studios, New York.*

A PRACTICAL FORM OF CAVALLETTI

This is the kind of ruggedly constructed cavalletto the team uses at its training headquarters on the Greenwich, Connecticut, estate of Mr. Alvin Untermyer. Two sets of cavalletti have been laid out parallel to each other, the far ones placed in a slightly shorter distance than the near set in order to accommodate the shorter stride of smaller horses. Plain rails on the ground serve almost as well, but the ease with which they are displaced is annoying unless there is a helper on foot who can reset them. *Photo: Budd Studios, New York.*

MORTON W. ("CAPPY") SMITH RIDING HIS WIFE'S
JAZZ SESSION AT WARRENTON

Few riders can equal Cappy Smith in holding together a "wandery" sort of green
horse, or driving a roguish horse or a tired horse around a big course, and this picture
shows why: Cappy has Jazz Session well up in the bridle and completely before his
strong seat. His forward inclination is no more than an exact response to the effort
Jazz Session has made over this little fence, and the over-all picture is one of great
strength of position along with beautiful balance. If we should ask, "Where would
Cappy end up sitting if Jazz Session should stumble on landing?" our answer would
be, "Just about where he's sitting now." *Photo: Budd Studios, New York.*

RAYMOND BURR RIDING KIMBERTON HILL FARM'S KIMBERTON VIKE AT HARRISBURG

Raymond Burr seems instantly able to adapt his riding to almost any type of horse, and he is one of the very few riders who really look equally at home on hunters, jumpers, and chasers. His seat is basically orthodox, enabling him to exercise a subtle control of balance without indulging in any of the gymnastics so many jumper riders feel compelled to employ. In this picture Vike is reaching for a spread fence which he has met rather "long"; Raymond has given him every encouragement to extend, yet without having committed himself in a way that would have jeopardized his own safety had Vike cheated at the take-off or made more of a dive at the fence. *Photo: Budd Studios, New York.*

ROBERT BURKE RIDING MRS. WINSTON GUEST'S CAMEDA AT DEVON

Even on high-strung horses Bobby always seems relaxed and almost casual on a hunter course, riding with a long rein and encouraging his horses to move freely. Blessed with an excellent eye for distance and a finely developed sense of "equestrian tact," Bobby is a master at finessing and camouflaging difficult moments and usually seems, as in this picture, to be simply enjoying himself on a horse that is carrying him kindly. *Photo: Budd Studios, New York.*

JOE GREEN RIDING MR. W. R. BALLARD'S WINDSOR CASTLE

Joe was already a very successful jumper rider when I went to my first horse show, and this picture, taken some twenty-five years later, shows some of the elements that have helped him achieve a career of remarkably consistent success. Joe's very accurate eye and wonderful sense of pace and timing have brought Windsor Castle into this hog's back in exactly the right stride, leaving Joe little to do but permit him enough freedom to extend his head and neck. Joe's position isn't quite what one would call classic, but the sense of balance is very much there, and the proof of the pudding is in Windsor Castle's virtually perfect bascule. *Photo: Budd Studios, New York.*

MISS ELIZABETH BOSLEY RIDING THE CLOWN AT PIPING ROCK

An all-round horsewoman, "Miss Boz" is quite as much at home on a race horse or a hunter as the jumper we see her on here. Blessed with a wonderful natural co-ordination and sense of timing, Betty has never had to develop a particularly scientific approach to riding; usually she just does what comes naturally to her, and most often this proves to have been just the right thing to do. In this picture the horse's thrust in leaving the ground has slightly displaced Betty's lower leg, but once more the relationship between centers of gravity is perfect and the degree of support by the hand exactly right. *Photo: Budd Studios, New York.*

MRS. EDWARD HOGAN RIDING MISS ELEANORA SEARS'S SIDONIA IN MADISON SQUARE GARDEN

Mrs. Hogan (or Joanie Walsh, as most horse-show people still think of her) demonstrates brilliantly how little strength alone has to do with riding. The daughter of a great jumper rider who became one of the leading American steeple-chase trainers, Joanie can ride just about anything that comes with four legs, and though she rides at a real jockey's weight, somehow nothing ever seems to be taking much hold of her. Some of the prettiest schools I have ever seen a chaser turn in were ridden by Joanie, and some of the smoothest hunter rounds as well. The feeling of ease and poised relaxation in the picture above is very characteristic—and very hard to improve on. *Photo: Budd Studios, New York.*

F. D. ("DOOLEY") ADAMS RIDING MRS. OGDEN PHIPPS'S OEDIPUS
AT SARATOGA, 1953

    I have always considered Dooley Adams in a class by himself among postwar American steeplechase riders. Equipped with wonderful physical skills and a keen analytical intelligence, Dooley combined these ingredients into a style that was both effective and elegant—the lovely feeling of balance and poise in the picture above is typical. Another well-rounded horseman, Dooley felt that his race riding benefited materially from his experience with other forms of riding; in the same way, I feel that the show jumper can learn much of value from galloping race horses and carefully observing the best riders in all other branches of equestrian sport. *Photo: Bert Morgan, New York.*

GENERAL HUMBERTO MARILES (MEXICO) RIDING ARETE IN
WEMBLEY STADIUM, LONDON, 1948
(Olympic Gold Medal, 1948)

There is a common misconception that only the rider who is "making a lot of moves" is "really trying"; and, in fact, one of the hardest things for a rider to do is to refrain from overriding the key fences in the most important competitions. The picture above is an example of superb composure as well as superb equilibrium, for it shows General Mariles jumping the last fence in the 1948 Olympic Games—the fence that assured him of winning the Gold Medal—with a confident freedom from extraneous moves that would have passed for nonchalance on a lesser occasion!
Photo: J. Bridel, L'Année Hippique-Paddock, Lausanne.

PIERRE JONQUÈRES D'ORIOLA (FRANCE) RIDING ALI BABA AT THE PARC DES PRINCES, PARIS

(Olympic Gold Medal, 1952)

Pierrot has left at this big oxer from rather far back, on a long stride, and the picture shows him concerned more with encouraging a good "follow through" over the fence than maintaining contact, which has been very slightly lost. His balance is a bit forward, which is just where I would like it under the circumstances; if he were sitting farther back, with a more erect upper body, I would probably wonder if the horse might not hit the fence behind during his descent. *Photo: O. Cornaz, L'Année Hippique-Paddock, Lausanne.*

FRANCESCO ("PACO") GOYOAGA (SPAIN) RIDING FAHNENKÖNIG
AT AACHEN   (World Champion, 1953)

Paco's riding has always been characterized by tremendous drive, and, looking at
this picture, I have the feeling that he could drive a horse through a brick wall from
this position. The seat is very strong, and Paco has just folded up instead of pushing
forward so that he remains right in the middle of the horse. With all his drive, Paco
always gives a horse a place to go—forward—and his hands are beautiful here, permitting the horse to express with his bascule all the impulsion created during the
approach. *Photo: O. Cornaz, L'Année Hippique-Paddock, Lausanne.*

MAJOR HENRI ST. CYR (SWEDEN) RIDING MARQUIS AT AACHEN,
1959   (Olympic Gold Medal, Dressage, 1952, 1956)
This is a wonderful seat; every time I look at this picture I am struck by the
wonderful elasticity of St. Cyr's back, and the description "he looks glued on"
comes to mind. The horse's impulsion and liveliness are clearly manifest, and the
evident security of St. Cyr's position seems to derive entirely from its harmoniousness
and balance rather than from any muscular effort on his part. *Photo: O. Cornaz,
L'Année Hippique-Paddock, Lausanne.*

SERGEI FILATOV (U.S.S.R.) RIDING ABSENT, ROME, 1960
(Olympic Gold Medal, Dressage, 1960)

This is a rather delicate moment for Filatov, for Absent has started his passage too much on the forehand and is trying to "take" his rider's hand. Filatov has refused to respond to this resistance by pulling, but instead is lightening the forehand by slightly raising his hand (note the subtle break in the line from the bit to his elbow) and insisting on the movement "from behind" with a strong leg and back. The rider can never overcome a tendency toward rigidity in the horse by becoming more rigid himself, but only by intensifying his driving stimuli; the very vital, elastic feeling of Filatov's back suggests that this is precisely his endeavor. *Photo: O. Cornaz, L'Année Hippique-Paddock, Lausanne.*

HANS GÜNTER WINKLER (GERMANY) RIDING HALLA AT NICE
(Olympic Gold Medal, 1956; World Champion, 1954, 1955)

Hans's wonderful accuracy in riding approaches enables him to leave the ground with little to do except maintain equilibrium, and his position in the air usually shows more emphasis on delicacy of contact than on security, as here. The feeling of movement is extremely free and harmonious, and while the leg is not in a strong position, Halla's great natural impulsion makes it possible for Hans to regulate her forward movement with only the lightest of leg aids. This combination has an astonishing record in winning the most important competitions, reflecting a very delicately balanced relationship between two high-strung and intensely competitive temperaments. *Photo: O. Cornaz, L'Année Hippique-Paddock, Lausanne.*

HANS GÜNTER WINKLER RIDING FEUERDORN AT AACHEN, 1960

Hans likes his young horses to develop a self-reliant and soundly orthodox way of going in their first year or two of showing, and exercises great discretion and patience in establishing this sound foundation. Here he is "helping" Feuerdorn only by sitting perfectly still and perfectly balanced on him as he jumps up onto Aachen's small "*Wegesprung*" bank. *Photo: Theodor Janssen*

FRITZ THIEDEMANN (GERMANY) RIDING FINALE AT AACHEN
(Champion of Europe, 1958)

Fritz's workmanlike, durable style has accounted for more wins on more different horses since the war than any other rider in Germany. Like most riders who have ridden a lot of young horses, Fritz rarely commits his body very far forward and likes to keep his horses very much in front of him. In emergencies he will sit almost anywhere the situation seems to demand and will not consent for a moment to "being taken." This beautiful jump shows Fritz right in the middle of the horse, where he likes to be, in a position that combines great security with perfect balance, and Finale is putting her knees exactly where we would always like to see them. *Photo: O. Cornaz, L'Année Hippique-Paddock, Lausanne.*

CAPTAIN PIERO D'INZEO (ITALY) RIDING THE ROCK AT THE
PIAZZA DI SIENA, ROME
(Champion of Europe, 1959; Olympic Silver Medal, 1960)
Behind the smooth and apparently effortless performances Piero achieves in the
ring lies an enormous capacity for concentrated work at home, and a very clear
conception of how he wants his horses to go. Piero's horses always seem to be
meeting their fences going forward, and our picture shows him in complete
equilibrium with a horse who is obviously "before his seat." *Photo: O. Cornaz,
L'Année Hippique-Paddock, Lausanne.*

CAPTAIN RAIMONDO D'INZEO (ITALY) RIDING POSILIPPO AT THE
PARC DES PRINCES, PARIS, 1959
(Olympic Gold Medal, 1960; World Champion, 1956, 1960)
Posilippo has left the ground at this oxer on a rather short stride, and Raimondo
is offering him every encouragement to round his back and carry out over the
fence. I have heard this kind of position criticized for not being completely "classic,"
but for me the feeling is so just, and the balance so in keeping with the horse's
effort, that there is nothing I would like to change. *Photo: Budd Studios, New York.*

CAPTAIN RAIMONDO D'INZEO RIDING THE QUIET MAN AT AACHEN

This remarkable picture shows Raimondo winning the Puissance at Aachen in 1958, jumping 2.16 meters—over 7 feet—with his right arm in a cast. The Quiet Man has met this huge wall with very good impulsion off a short stride, and Raimondo is giving him complete freedom to "break himself in two" over the fence, his own balance beautifully related to the horse's. Raimondo's ability to adapt his riding to widely divergent types of horses—Posilippo and The Quiet Man, Merano and Hack On—reflects an insight into the range of equine temperament that few riders will ever match. *Photo: O. Cornaz, L'Année Hippique-Paddock, Lausanne.*

PAT SMYTHE (ENGLAND) RIDING FLANAGAN AT LUCERNE, 1960
(European Women's Champion, 1958)

Pat has been able to present Flanagan to this fence exactly the way she wanted to, and she has nothing to do now but sit quietly and very delicately preserve the balance that was created during the approach. Pat's brilliant record of competitive success is a tribute both to her tenacious competitive temperament and her sound technique and demonstrates again that show jumping is a sport in which women can compete on very level terms with men. *Photo: O. Cornaz, L'Année Hippique-Paddock, Lausanne.*

MYSELF ON DEMOCRAT IN MADISON SQUARE GARDEN IN 1952
Democrat was probably the most generous horse I ever rode, and the privilege of riding him during the "fall circuit" of Harrisburg-New York-Toronto in 1952 was one of the most treasured experiences of my riding career. Assigned to me as a "second" horse to back up Hollandia, my mount in the 1952 Games, Democrat challenged that status despite his nineteen years and proceeded to win every individual class we showed him in throughout the three shows—eight in all. What should have been Democrat's best years coincided with the war, but his brilliant successes under Colonel F. F. Wing in 1941 and 1947–48 suggest that he would have compiled an international record more nearly commensurate with his remarkable gifts had his career developed normally. *Photo: Budd Studios, New York.*

HUGH WILEY RIDING HIS OWN NAUTICAL AT THE PENNSYLVANIA NATIONAL, 1959

Hugh and Nautical constitute one of those rare, happy combinations in which the rider's natural temperament and technique are perfectly related to the horse's best way of going. At its brilliant best, this pair can make the most difficult things look easy and possesses an extraordinary dramatic quality that has made it as popular with audiences abroad as those in the United States. In this interesting picture Nautical is reaching for the "out" of a very long two-combination, has started to twist a bit behind in his effort to avoid a fault. While Hugh is already sitting very well up on him, he has also reached forward with his outside hand to insure that he will not come back the slightest bit and will give Nautical every chance to follow through, a very healthy instinct in situations like this. *Photo: Budd Studios, New York.*

MYSELF SCHOOLING MRS. JOHN GALVIN'S NIGHT OWL, 1955

This photograph of Night Owl was taken rather early in his career, some five years before he won the coveted Grand Prix of Aachen under George Morris. It demonstrates exactly what I mean by "steadying a horse in the air," for Night Owl was apparently a shade strong in approaching this fence, and my hand, while in no way rigid or fixed, affords active support instead of merely following passively.

GEORGE MORRIS ON MR. WALTER DEVEREUX'S SINJON AT LONDON

Sinjon combines a miraculously elastic jumping mechanism with a rather difficult temperament that was probably not improved by his career as a race horse. It is a tribute to George's diplomatic instincts and delicate sense of balance that this temperamental volatility is so little in evidence in Sinjon's show-ring performances, and this picture shows George's talents in action: he has refused to "sit against" this lively little horse but has him very nicely balanced between the discreet supports of hand and leg, and the whole picture is marked by an evident sympathy and harmony between horse and rider.

MYSELF ON MISS ELEANORA SEARS'S KSAR D'ESPRIT
AT LONDON, 1958

I think that this is really quite an extraordinary picture, for Ksar has left the ground quite a long way away from this oxer and is still "making it look easy." His wonderful freedom of shoulder has permitted him to put his knees right up under his chin without the slightest sign of desperation, and for once the sensation of flight seems truly preserved in a "still" picture. *Photo: Monty.*

FRANK CHAPOT RIDING HIS MARE, GAY HARMONY, AT AACHEN, 1960

Frank has always especially enjoyed the challenge that speed classes afford to save ground and "make shifty moves"—and here we see him gambling against the clock on Gay Harmony and saving a second or two by continuing his turn in the air. His position could hardly be better, for he has lost no fraction of balance or control and remains precisely in the middle of his horse so that he will be able to complete his turn and continue to the next fence with no loss of cadence or impulsion. *Photo: Theodor Janssen.*

MYSELF ON MISS JOAN MAGID'S FIRST BOY AT AACHEN, 1958

First Boy was not always an easy horse to ride, for he was very highly strung temperamentally, and little things often had a way of upsetting him. At his best he was capable of really brilliant rounds, however, as on the night at London in 1956 when he achieved the distinction of bringing the George V Gold Cup back to our shores for the first time in some twenty-five years and won for me the honor of receiving the trophy from Queen Elizabeth II herself. *Photo: Guido Wedding, Essen.*

(At right)
MYSELF ON MISS ELEANORA SEARS'S KSAR D'ESPRIT
AT ROTTERDAM, 1958

"Ksarro" has his personal idiosyncracies too, and the fact that he sometimes finds small fences boring is one of them. How grateful I have been to him for knowing just what to do with the big ones, however! In the picture above he is taking me quite unconcernedly over the biggest fence I had ever ridden at up to that time, Rotterdam's Puissance wall set at just over seven feet. Since then Ksar has taken me over almost a dozen very big Puissance walls, and I know that if my life depended on jumping one of them tomorrow, I would only hope to see it looming larger between those wise gray ears of his. *Photo: Ary Groeneveld.*

MYSELF ON MR. & MRS. BERNIE MANN'S RIVIERA WONDER
AT AACHEN, 1960

"Wonder" names are much commoner than wonder horses, but I'd happily defend the appropriateness of the name in this case; I've never ridden a horse who could do more different kinds of difficult things more easily. I doubt that any horse will ever equal Wonder's record of four National Horse Show Championships, and his defeat of the best horses in Europe in the German International Championship of 1959 showed that his versatile talents suffered no loss in transit across the ocean. All in all, Wonder's combination of physical structure and jumping instincts comes the closest to my personal ideals of any horse I've known. In the picture above, Wonder is jumping out a very long two-combination, and making it appear very easy indeed. *Photo: Theodor Janssen.*

ance while lengthening and shortening his stride at all gaits.

The element of temperamental equilibrium is of crucial importance to successful jumping. Since strength and flexibility are functions of relaxation and not of uncontrollable tension, a calm, confident, emotionally stable attitude toward jumping is essential for both the horse and rider. I have often felt that most riders, and in consequence, the horses they ride, tend to consistently overestimate the aggregate of speed and impulsion that is necessary to negotiate an obstacle of a given height. The less experienced rider is far more likely to override the larger fences on the course than to ride them too weakly, and quite often we witness moments of real panic during the last two or three strides. The rider must overcome any temperamental compulsion to hurry, and should remember that it is possible in even the most desperate situation to simply make a circle and approach the fence again.

The technique of simplifying problems in degree while maintaining their characteristic kind is just as basic to schooling over fences as it is to schooling on the flat. The jump, reduced to its simplest form, is simply the rail on the ground, or the low *cavalletto*,[1] and thus rails and *cavalletti* play an important role in our training of the jumper. (Since they are so frequently used, it is worth the trouble to make a set of special *cavalletti*; they are less easily displaced by a slight tick, and not quite so much liberty can be taken with them. Moreover, their slight elevation—a total height of 8 inches is enough—not

---

[1] *Cavalletto* (*cavalletti* in the plural) is the Italian word for "little horse"; it refers to what we might term a little sawhorse, a rail that is supported by small wooden x's or blocks affixed to each end.

only demands a little more thinking on the part of the horse, but also develops his jumping muscles more quickly.)

The best place to start teaching the green horse or the spoiled horse the fundamentals of jumping is with the simplest possible obstacle, and our work will commence with a single rail on the ground, or *cavalletto*, taken at a walk. When this lesson has been learned quite thoroughly, the rider can commence trotting over the rail, and also walking through a short series of *cavalletti*. At this early stage, the spacing of the *cavalletti* should be adjusted to the particular horse's stride. The obstacles should be negotiated with no alteration of stride and no change in pace whatsoever; it is not the rider's function to "place" his horse at these tiny obstacles, but only to maintain balance and impulsion.

As the horse learns to negotiate a series of *cavalletti* at a normal trot, with perfect evenness of gait and equanimity of temperament, the rider can gradually lengthen the spacing, keeping it always even, and can then add a small obstacle—perhaps 3 feet in height—following the *cavalletti*, to be negotiated in the same cadence. (The average distance between *cavalletti* will vary between 5 and 6 feet, and the correct spacing for the fence following *cavalletti* will be 11 or 12 feet. Should the rider be tempted to shorten the spacing beyond these minimums, it will probably be because he has not taught his horse to trot with sufficient impulsion.)

With the warning that no more difficult work should be attempted until the execution of this basic exercise is absolutely perfect, all pains should be taken to maintain the horse's interest during this kind of gymnastic exercise, and innumerable variations are possible. The type of fence that follows the *cavalletti* may be varied, small oxers being particularly appropriate, and low combinations can be built following the first obstacle.

Good horses and riders are capable of jumping quite sizable fences after the regularized approach that is furnished by the *cavalletti*; but while the good pupil may be able to jump fences in the range of 4 feet to 4 feet 6 quite easily from a trot, the emphasis should be on varying the type and spacing of fences more than their height.

When a series of low obstacles is used following the *cavalletti*, the horse will benefit much from slight variations or its distances that make him alternately extend or shorten his stride; for example, if the fence following the *cavalletti* is a 3-foot-3-inch oxer spread 3 feet, the following obstacle might be a vertical fence in a rather short distance, the next fence another low oxer in a slightly longer distance, and the final fence a vertical fence, perhaps a little higher, in a short distance again. (In this example, I have in mind one-stride distances, which would be something between 21 and 24 feet, but an alternation of one-stride and two-stride distances (31 to 39 feet) will also be found very instructive.)

While *cavalletti* are extremely useful in developing the horse's jumping mechanism and the rider's co-ordination, the lessons learned with the assistance of this training aid must be carried over to the negotiation of low fences without preparatory *cavalletti*, so that both horse and rider can begin to acquire an "eye for distances." These fences should be about 3 feet 6 inches in height, and jumped both from a trot and a slow canter. *Cavalletti* work and

low single fences are the jumper's "scales"; just as the
beginner and the virtuoso musician both work on some of
the same basic exercises every day, so do the green jumper
and the Olympic star, and anyone who has watched our
Olympic team in training, or the German, or the Italian,
will know what an important part these simple technical
disciplines still play in the daily routine of such horses as
Nautical, Meteor, and The Rock.

The training field at home is the place to stress fundamentals, and never to be quite satisfied that they are
performed well enough. In daily work there is always time
to repeat an exercise, to concentrate on details, or to
isolate a particular aspect of a problem. Later on in the
show ring, the horse and rider will have so many other
things to think about that they must be able to do the
basic things correctly almost as second nature.

Concentrate on technique at home, so that your mind
will be free to concentrate on your performance as a
whole in the show ring. In other words, develop a technique
that will continue to function reliably even when you're
not watching it. Not a very easy recipe for success—heaven
knows, the ingredients take long enough to prepare—but
still, I don't know of a better one.

CHAPTER 7

Advanced
Schooling over Fences

Advanced Schooling over Fences

Although work over *cavalletti* and the small obstacles placed after them provides a good foundation on which to develop the horse's skills, it serves only as an introduction to the jumping of entire courses.

What kind of problems must we be able to deal with effectively when we start jumping courses? While every course will be different, we can classify the basic kinds of problems as follows.

First, there are the obstacles that can be ridden as completely separate fences. The first fence on the course, at which one makes an entirely fresh start, falls into this category, as does almost every fence that initiates a new line. In addition, fences that are more than six or seven strides apart may usually be ridden as separate fences, since the distance between them provides sufficient space for major alterations in the horse's stride.

Second, there are the fences in long related distances. (The three- to six-stride distances—40 to 80 feet—may be called "related" because the manner in which the horse negotiates the first fence will have a definite bearing on his approach to the second fence.)

Third, there are the combinations—doubles or trebles within a maximum distance of 39 feet, in which the approach to the first fence very directly determines the way the horse will meet the subsequent obstacles in the combination.

And fourth, there are turns.

All of these ingredients must be mastered separately before they are combined into the complex act of negotiating an entire course. All the different types of approaches that may be necessary must be within the grasp of the horse and rider, and the transitions between them must be prompt, obedient, and accurate.

Since *cavalletti* provide an aid in determining the correct take-off point which will not exist in the show ring, the ability to find consistently and accurately the right take-off at a single fence is probably the basic foundation for the more sophisticated skills that must be built on it. Trotting over a low single fence is perhaps the best simple exercise for developing this skill, for it discourages the most serious single fault of horses and riders—anticipation. Because I feel this is so important and so fundamental, I do not approve of the practice of starting at a trot, and then permitting the horse to slip into a canter at a point of his own choosing during the approach. If the fence cannot be negotiated directly from a trot, it should be lowered; and until the horse can be maintained in an even trot right up to the moment of take-off, the tendency to rush or to anticipate will always be there, waiting to be exposed by the exigencies of the show ring.

Although *cavalletti* work is extremely useful in preventing the tendency to rush, it may not suffice by itself. Here the rider will find circling in front of the fence of great value. I must warn that circling, if it is to prove effective, must be perfectly done: as the horse makes his circle he must come squarely and directly at the center of the fence, and the rider *must not* "telegraph" his intention as to whether he will jump the fence or circle to the right or to the left; in fact, he must not know himself which he is going to do until he has reached that point. Any imperfection in the horse's movement or carriage, even one which develops at the very last moment, must be corrected by circling; and even when the approach is perfect, the fence should not be jumped every time. (With the "hot" horse who is most likely to benefit from this exercise, the ratio of jumps to circles should probably never exceed one to three or four, and in the early stages, when the lesson is still to be learned, it may be necessary to make a dozen or more circles before the fence can be jumped once.) It is of paramount importance that the horse should never be able to anticipate the rider, and this means not only that the rider must refrain from attempting to "lift" the horse as he leaves the ground, but also that he must ensure there is not the slightest difference between the approach that precedes a jump and the approach that precedes another circle.

The idea seems to persist even among very experienced riders that *some* activity on the part of the rider is necessary at the instant the horse leaves the ground. This tenacious idea is also an extremely harmful one, for it requires the rider to time very precisely actions that are really quite unnecessary. For a long time this was my idea, too. I really didn't believe that a horse was capable of leaving the ground without some "move"—at least a little one—on my part. "He's bigger than you are—don't try to carry him, make him carry you" is advice that still rings in my memory, uttered with increasing impatience by Morton ("Cappy") Smith on a series of hot summer afternoons some years ago. Finally I learned, and I am still grateful to him for having hammered into me this very sound advice.

Correctly, the rider does absolutely *nothing* as the horse leaves the ground. It is my view that nothing is necessary— not even a little extra relaxation, or a little extra leg pressure. If the rider's position during the approach is sound, which is to say, if he is in balance, the thrust of the horse as he begins his flight will automatically close the rider's angles. Ideally, he will only maintain the contact with the horse's mouth that was necessary during the approach.

There is another form of anticipation that is almost as harmful as that which comes from trying to time some combination of movements or gestures with the horse's take-off and jump: the anticipation of the approach. One of the commonest mistakes is that of trying to create all the impulsion and speed that is going to be required to jump the fence within one stride of heading for it—a kind of premature "winding-up" of the horse. I do not wish to imply that the rider should make a haphazard approach or only improvise his preparations as he goes along; his length of rein and his position, and his horse's balance and carriage should be established before he starts to ride to the first fence, and maintained for the entire series of fences that has to be jumped. But from this start, he should proceed gradually to establish the pace and degree of impulsion he needs.

The whole process should consist of a fluid development, culminating in the jump itself, and at no point should the rider have the feeling that there is a hurry to get there, or a necessity to go before his horse has gone. One of the characteristic feelings one gets in watching good riders—or indeed good performers in any activity—is that they are unhurried, that they always have plenty of time. The tendency to anticipate the horse and to seem to "leave without him," as it were, is particularly dangerous because of its bad effect on the horse's temperament. Most very "hot" and rapid horses develop that pattern because of impatient riders who anticipate the approach. The tendency to rush can often be corrected, but it is much better to prevent such a pattern from ever developing.

If the idea that the rider must do something to initiate the jump is a pernicious one, so is the practical application many riders make of the concept of the "following hand." Quite often we see—especially in horsemanship classes— riders abandoning all support by the hand as the horse leaves the ground in the idea that they are doing something that is right, even though it goes against their instinct. Their horses will usually jump one or two fences quite nicely, but often are flying by the time they reach the last fence. (To be sure, this is not so serious a sin as that of bothering the horse's mouth by coming back, or seriously impeding the downward extension of the head and neck during the take-off; but it is just as important to avoid the danger of a sudden *withdrawal* of support of the hand as it is to avoid the sudden intervention of the hand.)

In other words, the correct "following hand" follows by maintaining the same degree of contact with the horse's mouth, no matter how great (or how little, in the case of small fences) the extension of the head and neck may be. It is clear that if this goal is to be achieved, the rider's hands and arms must be completely independent from his body and his seat, and must play no part in maintaining his position.

I am certain that in the early stages of learning how to jump, holding on to the mane or martingale is both desirable and practical. For the occasional rider, this expedient may have a usefulness that continues long beyond his novice stage, to be relied on in emergencies, whenever there is danger that he may come back, or that he may interfere with the horse's mouth. It is, however, an expedient, and until the rider's position has become so secure that the hands play no role whatsoever in his support, there will be subtle degrees of balance that will be impossible for him to maintain.

The best way I know of developing a completely independent seat over fences is to ride a well-trained horse down a chute, or in a corral, absolutely without reins, and with the hands clasped behind the back, or on top of the rider's head, or simply extended from the shoulders at right angles.

Jumping with reins but without stirrups is probably less helpful, for it encourages the rider to conceal momentary losses of balance by using his hands. Nevertheless, it does help to strengthen the seat, and it also tends to discourage the habits of anticipating. (In horsemanship classes, the ride-off over fences without stirrups rarely seems to produce a conclusive result, for all of the children tend to ride very much better under these circumstances.)

The above discussion of the role of the hand in jumping—the maintenance of the contact established during the approach—applies to normal circumstances. Most books on riding somehow neglect to mention what should be done under *abnormal* circumstances, and unfortunately these occur quite frequently in our riding experience too. Under abnormal circumstances there are times to increase contact, and times to lose contact altogether.

First there is the horse who has no reluctance to drop his head and neck during the jump but is anxious for temperamental reasons to "pick up speed in the air." It is really dangerous to turn this kind of horse's head loose as he leaves the ground, and he should, if anything, be steadied a bit *more* in the air. Not by a jab, of course, or a rigid hand, but by a very gradual and steady increase in the support of the hand. Even the sensible horse must sometimes be steadied a bit more as he takes off, as, for example, when he has made too bold an approach over the first fence of a combination that is going to ride short; or when, for reasons of freshness, he wants to hurry in jumping small fences or vertical fences.

This is perhaps dangerous advice, for the steadier hold must be applied with very great skill and discretion, and must never reach a point that endangers the horse's bascule (the rounding of his back in flight). "Contact, contact, contact" is always the riding master's cry, but there are also circumstances under which, as a practical matter, I think it is quite permissible and even desirable to lose contact with the horse's mouth altogether. If a horse has missed his take-off, and is struggling to reach a fence from a very long stand-back, or with a spoiled or timid horse who tends to "dwell" over his fences and is afraid to extend, I am quite happy to see the rider give him complete freedom of his head. With green or timid or spoiled horses who are afraid of their mouths, actual contact in the air must be established slowly and carefully, and it may be some time before the horse gains sufficient confidence in the steadiness and generosity of the rider's hand to permit the lightest contact during the jump. This confidence is both a precious and a fragile thing—guard it wisely!

Routine, and the boredom and carelessness that often accompany it, must always be avoided in the training of the jumper. Fences should always be varied—if not from day to day, at least several times during the week, and all kinds of obstacles, in miniature, should be employed. They need not exceed 3 feet 6 inches in height, but they should represent all the kinds of obstacles the horse will meet in the show ring—small oxers, triple bars, oil drums, and so forth.

Small spread fences should teach both the horse and the rider the correct technique of jumping this type of obstacle. The best way to ride at spread fences is to create sufficient impulsion (impulsion, and not speed)—and wait. Wait—for the stand-back makes the spread fence, which is already wide, even wider. Thus the rider's aim should be to make his take-off at the closest possible point that still permits the horse to elevate quickly enough to clear the first rail.

Low fences are also the place to start teaching the horse to jump fences at angles. The approach should always be very steady, and straight along the line the rider has chosen. This should be on only a slight bias at first, but the well-trained horse who has learned to trust and obey his rider should be capable of approaching and negotiating fences on quite an acute angle. Later on, this ability will prove useful many times, not only in speed classes where the ability to jump fences at an angle is an essential means of saving time, but even in regular classes where an abnormally close take-off can often be salvaged by angling the fence at the last moment, and gaining a few precious extra feet of take-off room.

Up to now I have not mentioned the problem of refusals or run-outs, for if the rider proceeds patiently and methodically, and conquers the impulse to overextend the green horse or the badly trained horse, he should have few such problems. Most refusals derive, it seems to me, not from any stubbornness on the horse's part, but simply from his recognition that he has reached a point from which a good jump is impossible. The upset horse, the horse who knows that he must drag his rider with him as he leaves the ground, the horse who has been given too little impulsion, or pace, or the wrong balance, may very likely stop, and he is often right in doing so. Under these circumstances, he should not be punished, but the deficiency should be corrected and the fence rejumped.

The green horse, too, is likely to make a fuss about new and strange obstacles—and almost everything will be new and strange to him. He should be given ample time to explore and smell and examine new fences, and then very firmly asked to jump them. If he is asked confidently and firmly, and is not asked to do unreasonable things, he will learn to come to fences, even strange ones, with no more than a healthy curiosity as to how he is to negotiate them. And this is the attitude that must be developed.

In many senses, the role of the rider is very much like the role of the parent. The overly severe parent often creates not well-disciplined children, but criminals and neurotics. The overly permissive rider produces very much the same result as the overly permissive parent: a horse who never learns to accept his own responsibilities and who feels licensed to stop, and explore, and indulge himself whenever he encounters the slightest thing that is new or strange.

It is unfortunate that some of the nicest people, with the deepest and most genuine sympathy for horses, completely frustrate their own pleasures and ruin the horses they ride by unreasonable indulgence.

On the whole, a moment's thought about the parallel with children will suggest the wisest course of action in dealing with disobedience. Never nag, and never punish confusion or ignorance. Punishment, when it is necessary, whether with the leg, the whip, or the voice, should be prompt and definite, and of short duration. When correction is applied in this way, the need for it will diminish quite rapidly.

The only horse to whom the above recommendations do not apply is the rogue—the equine equivalent of the congenitally criminal personality. As in the case of humans, some rogues are so gifted that we are tempted to take the enormous pains they require in hopes that they can be redeemed. Almost by definition, this is impossible with the real rogue, and as a rider's experience expands, he will begin to learn the telltale gestures and expressions that distinguish the rogue, or the genuinely dishonest horse, from the various spoiled and frightened horses that present some of the same symptoms. When a true rogue is encountered, the best advice is probably to dispose of him, no matter how beautiful he is, or how wonderfully he can go "when he wants to." However, such horses are very rare—and should a rider find that he is encountering very many truly stubborn, or unwilling, or dishonest temperaments, he should examine his own skills and find what it is that he is doing that has made him such a bad horseman. For one of the great delights of riding lies in the enormous generosity and willingness to forgive and forget that the vast majority of horses hand to us as a gift.

CHAPTER 8

Preparations for the Horse Show

Preparations for the Horse Show

The basic foundations of riding and schooling apply equally, of course, to schooling for the horse show, the hunt, or simply the cross-country ride. But if we can now take it for granted that the most fundamental considerations are already clearly understood, it may be helpful to consider the particular aspects of riding and schooling that apply particularly to the period immediately preceding competition.

Probably the most useful single suggestion I can make involves no change in the content or performance of the horse's schooling whatever—it is simply this: Define your objectives at the start.

Why do we compete in horse shows, anyway? Is it the camaraderie with other exhibitors that attracts us, the excitement of the competitive atmosphere, or the balm to the ego that a few good ribbons and a line or two in the press can afford? Or do we look forward to the show because it provides an opportunity to observe the experts in our division in action, and to compare their solutions to the problems that face us with our own? Probably the motivation of any single exhibitor is a very complex thing, composed of many elements.

In my own case, it is partly because the horse shows provide a good excuse to continue schooling, rather than being the end that justifies the time spent with horses at home. For my real interest lies in the educational development of the horse, which is accomplished primarily in his daily work; the horse show, like the school ex-amination, serves more as a periodic measurement of the state of the horse's and rider's development. I don't mean to suggest that I am uncompetitive, but it's probably true that my attitude is not essentially competitive; the personal challenge, matching of myself and my horse against the goals I have set for us during the show, is probably more important to me than the success, or lack of it, that I experience in terms of placing. In any case, I have won some classes which pleased me little and lost some classes in which my horses delighted me with the progress they showed. I have been told that this is not a particularly "healthy" attitude, but it is an inherent part of my own definition of horse show objectives. It is not at all a matter of not caring about winning; it is simply that I do not believe that the immediate win must always be the dominant goal, irrespective of its price.

With the horse whose education is not yet complete, there are many objectives at the horse show to choose between. With a jumper in particular, there is often a choice between the near-term goal—this particular class, which we may be able to win if we "crack" for it—and our long-range goal—the kind of horse we hope ours may be by the end of the season, and in years to come. The temptation to win the class at hand is strong, and it must be admitted that many of the long-term "waiters" somehow *never* seem to find the right moment to crack, not this year, or next, or the year after. But it is also certainly true that many of our most gifted horses never achieve their full potential because of damage done by being overmatched early in their careers.

More than once a nice young horse has caught my eye in the first class of a show, going confidently and well, and making only the odd "green" fault. Perhaps by the end of the afternoon, he has won some classes; but if the ribbons have been won at the expense of "standing him on his head" over a schooling fence, in order to "make him try harder," in this single afternoon most of the great early promise may be almost irretrievably destroyed. The commonest justification given for such tactics by some professionals is that "The owners insist on it—they want to see results, and if you can't get quick results, they'll look for another rider." But I have often wondered how many of these riders have ever really attempted to explain to their owners the consequences of the choice they make.

What I am building up to is the importance—especially with green horses—of being more concerned with *how* he goes than with where he finishes. If his progress is steady enough in regard to the way he goes and the variety of

problems he learns to solve in the show ring, the reward
in the form of ribbons will come far more surely, and
far more plentifully, than when the ribbons are sought too
soon and as an end in themselves.

With this in mind, we should enter the green horse,
during his first shows, in the classes from which he can
learn the most, and learn the right kind of thing; very
often, these will be green hunter or green working hunter
classes, rather than classes in the jumper division. With
the more mature campaigner, no such choice exists, of
course—he will go in his proper division. Presuming that
our horse is properly entered, and the tasks to be demanded
of him in the show ring are within the grasp of his
current standard of education, showing will be a question
of delivering in the show ring his best efforts.

What, then, can be done during the preparation for a
show to enable the horse to achieve his highest possible
standard of performance in the show ring? Three components will be involved: a technical one, concerning the
number of things the horse knows how to do; a physical
one, concerning his degree of fitness and stamina; and a
psychological one, concerning the attitude or frame of
mind with which he will enter the show ring.

If the show has been intelligently selected, and the
horse is really ready to be shown in the classes for which
he has been entered, the first consideration should pose
no special problems for the rider. The final schools will
merely continue to emphasize the weakest areas of the
horse's particular stage of preparation. If a kind of panicky
drilling seems required in the last few days before the
show, the rider should probably either skip the show
altogether, or use it to achieve only limited objectives, such

as letting the horse become familiar with the atmosphere of the show and the strange surroundings away from home.

In terms of psychological and physical preparation, the horse not only should be fit enough to meet the demands that will be made on him but also should have a little physical and mental edge of freshness. I don't mean that he should be unrideably fresh, or so "high" that all distractions would be magnified, but on the other hand he should certainly not have been jaded by a couple of long and unpleasant schooling sessions immediately preceding the show. From both the mental and physical points of view, it is probably better for a day's rest and a preceding day's light work to have been the preparation for the show than two days of long, serious work.

In other words, the best advice for schooling immediately before the show is simply "Don't panic." On average, I have found it best to work normally until within, say, four days of the show. On the fourth preceding day, the rider may well do a little more work than normally, concentrating particularly on weak spots for the young horse, and for the older horse perhaps jumping once or twice a larger course than the average height of the show. The third preceding day should be a sharp, but short résumé of the preceding day's work—a sort of preliminary test of what has been accomplished. For the old horse, this will simply mean jumping a few quite big fences, and perhaps a combination or two; for the younger horse, it will be an attempt to reproduce, in a short period of time, the best level of success attained the previous day. The second preceding day should be devoted to pleasant and relaxing work, aimed at reviving the horse's freshness of attitude and interest. The last day before the show is usually "shipping day" if the show is not too far away, and it will be quite enough, after the horse has arrived, to let him make an exploration of the show ground on a lead shank and pick a little grass.

When schooling over the outside course or in the ring is permitted before the show opens, the exhibitor will of course avail himself of this privilege. But the rider should do no more than give his horse a chance to orient himself and overcome any apprehensions about a new set of fences—it is *not* the time to try to remake the horse.

These suggestions are largely self-evident, and perhaps they will seem naïve to some readers, for they seem to ignore the kind of "last school" that is probably the commonest—if least commonly discussed—among jumper exhibitors: the poling session.

Through the years, I have listened to countless discussions of the pros and cons of poling, and recognize full well what violent emotions are stirred in the hearts of many horse people whenever the subject is introduced. This is no doubt why most books on jumping either avoid the subject, or dismiss it with a few critical lines. Nonetheless, it remains very much one of the facts of the show jumper's life—I doubt that one jumper out of twenty finishes the season without getting "sharpened up" sometime, in some fashion—and so I must risk incurring the wrath of some of the more rabid disputants on the subject by exploring it here at some length.

Poling, like severe bits, sharp spurs, or even high collection, is simply another "razor in the monkey's hand." True, one can condemn all of these things in toto by arguing that they are likely to be done inexpertly, injudiciously, and perhaps cruelly by the majority of people who attempt to use them. I cannot deny that clever people are cleverer than less clever people, and that the latter outnumber the former. But be that as it may, some of the corrective techniques that come under the general heading of poling can accomplish, in the hands of a skillful and experienced horseman, results that are beneficial and almost indispensable, under certain circumstances.

Under present rules, the American Horse Shows Association permits poling only with a light taped bamboo pole, except in states whose laws prohibit any kind of poling at all; the Fédération Equestre Internationale permits only the use of a light iron pipe, placed directly on top of the fence. While these restrictions are reasonably well enforced on most show grounds, there remains a wide range of practices that are employed at home—tack poles, tack rails, the rail on pulleys or held by two men, and baling wire are the commonest. What do all these devices hope to achieve? The obvious answer is "more clean rounds." This hope is often frustrated in practice, for poling can produce results that range from excellent to atrocious, depending on the skill and discretion with which it is employed. Some forms of poling *can* correct faults in a horse's jumping form, and *can* renew the respect of the careless horse for his fences—but poling can also destroy a horse's confidence and turn him into a stopper or a lunatic.

Since a widespread practice may be presumed to reflect a wide-spread need, we may ask how this need originates. Often "the rules" are blamed, meaning the AHSA rules under which touches are scored against the jumper as well as knock-downs. (And in fact, touches also count

against the hunter if they are more than very occasional.)
It is also argued, in the same vein, that the F.E.I. rules,
under which "ticks" are not penalized, minimize or eliminate the necessity of poling. My own feeling is that well-
designed courses do more to minimize the necessity for
poling than any particular scoring system, for the well-
designed course will favor, in the nature of the challenges
it presents, the horse who is jumping in good form over
the horse whose form has been spoiled by excessive poling.

But even over well-designed courses, many exhibitors
will feel that they need to do some "sharpening up" before
they will have much chance of jumping any clear rounds,
and in fact they are usually right. For it is easy to forget
that *everything* we do with the jumper becomes, whether
we intend it or not, a part of his preparation for the
show ring, and along with the profitable habits that
are formed in daily schooling it is very common that
an unprofitable one is formed too: the horse learns that
it's not terribly important to jump fences absolutely clean.
Since it must be an accepted fact of the horse's life in
the show ring that fences *do* have to be respected, how
is this result to be achieved?

If this is to be done successfully, it will hardly be
achieved by the "poling session" that attempts to change
the horse's attitude all in one afternoon, by teaching him
on that day an opposite lesson to the one he learns
every other day. But life is awfully short to spend waiting
for that wonderful, rare creature, the horse who is born
with an instinct to jump everything clean.

What, then, *can* be done in schooling to develop a
horse who will try to jump clean? First, it must be
recognized that there is no form of poling which can

correct a faulty approach, and bad approaches cause far more faults than sheer carelessness. But what of the horse who is meeting his fences well, and jumping in reasonably good form, but is just not trying? The commonest ways of dealing with him, "throwing a rail at him," or putting a strand of baling wire over the top of the fence, are not very logical solutions, for the fence we want the horse to jump clean in the show ring isn't going to have any men standing around it, or a strand of wire over it, or any visible peculiarity at all.

In general, the poling techniques that involve a person are the least satisfactory, for aside from the fact that the person can be seen, there is also a great possibility of human error on his part. Manual rapping can be effective—done very skillfully and judiciously—both in correcting faults in jumping form and discouraging carelessness, but very, very few people are sufficiently expert to achieve these results; more often, it is done at the wrong time, or in the wrong place, or continued too long, and in the end produces results just opposite to those desired. Moreover, the presence of the person at the fence often forces the rider to change his style of approach—if he sits quietly, his horse is very likely to stop. And so he teaches his horse to jump fences that have a man standing by them very cautiously, if at all—but this is a new category of experience that is not clearly related to what happens in the show ring.

Wire and the light iron pipe are better, for they will not punish the horse for a perfect jump, and they eliminate the factor of human error. (The pipe that is offset on the near side of the fence, just even with the top rail, can be very helpful in correcting the horse who is careless about

bending his knees.) However, they too can usually be
seen by the horse, and if they are employed very often
he will learn to discriminate between fences that have
wire or a pipe near them and those that don't.

It remains to consider the simplest means of discouraging
carelessness, the solid fence and the tack rail. Solid fences
are often used by cavalry schools for schooling green
horses, and I can remember that General Mariles had
a very good set of them in Mexico City. They have
the important advantages of natural appearance, and
require no change in riding style, but they also have
serious disadvantages: they penalize the bad mistake very
severely—with a big knee, or perhaps even a fall, which
will require a long period of restoring confidence. Moreover, they are not readily changeable as to location and
appearance. These disadvantages are not so serious for the
cavalry which has a large supply of manpower and horse
power, but they are very great disadvantages for the
individual.

Pursuing our inquiry to the end, we must evaluate
the tack rail. The term has always seemed to me to have
a particularly sinister sound—but if some artificial aid
must be used to achieve the rather artificial end of absolutely
clean jumping, and we are not afraid to consider it dis-
passionately, it probably has the most to recommend
it. The normal rail that has been studded with small
and *very* short nails will never punish a correct jump, but
penalizes only carelessness. Furthermore, its appearance
is perfectly normal, it involves no human agency, and
requires no change at all in the rider's style. I have
never used it very much, and prefer to err on the side
of using too few rather than too many artificial aids;

but the few people I have observed who used it consistently seem to me to have produced the most satisfactory results.

In any case, I believe that the best results during the horse show itself will be achieved if there has been no necessity to employ "emergency measures" to change the horse's attitude during the last few schools before the show. The horse who is jumping confidently and in good form, and who is only occasionally careless, should be corrected whenever this carelessness develops, by jogging down over a solid fence that will sting him a bit, placing a pipe where the careless jump will cause him to rap himself, or using a tack rail. For the average horse, this should be quite enough, and for the exceptionally clean or sensitive horse, usually the tick itself will serve as its own correction.

As he completes his preparation for the show, the rider should take pains to equip himself with everything he might reasonably expect to need during the show itself. Last-minute improvisations and borrowing of tack or clothing will constitute minor annoyances at a time when the rider should be occupied solely with the task at hand. Particular attention should be paid to one's provisions for bad weather: there should be rain gear for both horse and rider, and always an extra pair of gloves that will afford a good purchase on slippery reins. Check your tack *before* you pack for the show, so that there will be time to renew frayed stitching in a girth or a keeper that has pulled loose, and time to replace worn billets or stirrup leathers. Be sure that your horse is properly shod; if you are showing outdoors, it will be wise to use shoes that are tapped for studs which can be varied according to the condition of the ground. I think it is always a wise precaution to use rubber bell boots for showing, even if you don't use them for schooling when the accidental "grab" is less likely, and it is good to have an extra pair—it is surprising how often bell boots are torn, and the degree of protection they afford can make all the difference between a successful show and a sound horse and another one of life's small tragedies.

Finally, when you put your horse on the van to go to the show, make sure that he is safely dressed for shipping— if you think enough of him to show him, you should think enough of him to protect him properly in the van. He should have a head guard, and a shipping halter that is either covered with sheepskin or at least wrapped with an old tail bandage to prevent chafing; a tail guard or a tail bandage; and shipping boots or bandages, set up really carefully so that they'll stay in place during the trip. Somehow horses never seem so helpless or dependent on us as when we see them dressed in their traveling clothes, getting on the van with the expression of a small boy going off to school for the first time. Unfortunately, too many of them get off at the other end looking even more forlorn, nose rubbed, tail rubbed, and bandages, if any, around their ankles. Take pains with all these details, for in many ways the large achievement is no more than the aggregate of a lot of small achievements, and if the preparation for the show has been thorough and sound, the horse and rider will be halfway to having a good show before the first class has even started.

CHAPTER 9

The Horse Show

The Horse Show

It may be only a dusty field behind someone's barn, or it may be opening day at Aachen with 50,000 people watching and the flags of a dozen nations flying—but whatever and wherever the show, by the time the exhibitor arrives he should know *why* he is there, and have clarified in his own mind his objectives in relation to the particular horses he will be riding and their stages of development. These objectives may vary considerably—but whether you are showing hunters or jumpers, green horses getting their first horse show experience or seasoned campaigners with a real chance at the championship, your basic attitude towards showing should be the same: in fairness both to yourself and the horses you ride, the show ring should witness only your very best efforts.

If you succeed in this, you will enjoy the principal

pleasure that showing affords, no matter where the judges happen to place you. And if you *are* to succeed in this, you must develop certain show ring habits that are repeated in every class, with no exceptions, no matter how experienced you are, or how tired or disgusted you may be.

Perhaps I can sum it up best with the suggestion, "Know what you are going to have to do, and allow yourself plenty of time to do it." "Time to do it" means more than simply being on time for the class (although too many exhibitors habitually neglect to observe even this rule); it means giving yourself time not only to *make* the class, but also to prepare your horse properly for it, to give some thought to the course, and to watch a few other performances and *still* be on time for your own round. I know that it seems terribly blasé to be able to stand at the in gate and ask "What's the course?" or "What kind of class is this, anyway?"—and few of us have not been guilty of this crime on some occasion or other. But be that as it may, this kind of nonchalance is highly unsportsmanlike and unfair, not only to the public and to the other competitors but also to your horse as well as to yourself.

Knowing the class conditions also implies knowing the rules you are competing under. You should carry a rule book with you, in the tack trunk or in the car, and personally verify any question that may be in your mind instead of relying on the sometimes very unreliable knowledge or memory of other exhibitors. (As a member of the American Horse Shows Assocation Jumper Rules Committee, I have often been astonished at the persistance with which questions are asked that have long since been answered in the rule book.) There is no excuse for the exhibitor who is ignorant of the current rules governing the divisions in which he competes, and it is a wise precaution to review the rule book at least once a year, rereading the paragraphs you are "sure" you know already as well as making certain that you understand all changes that have been invoked.

Knowing in detail the course you are to compete over may require some little time, especially if the exhibitors are not permitted to walk the course. I and the other members of our team have often been kidded for having become excessively "distance conscious" and forever analyzing numbers of strides and distances in combinations, etc. Basically, there is nothing complicated at all about analyzing courses—it is merely a way of simplifying your task. Done with a reasonable amount of common sense, this very slight effort, without any change in your riding ability or your horse's skills, can salvage perhaps 25 per cent of your classes a year and move them from the unsuccessful category into a successful category. I will deal with the subject of course analysis in more detail in the following chapter.

Presuming that these obvious things can be taken for granted, most of the exhibitor's success or lack of it in the show ring will depend upon the soundness of his judgment. Two principal kinds of judgment are required by the horse show competitor—the judgment involved in deciding what one is going to try to do, and that which is involved in executing it.

Under the first category come such decisions as the type of round one suspects is most likely to find favor with the hunter judge, or which classes best justify one's maximum efforts. The idea that you can't "go in there

and give your all" every time the gate opens sometimes
disturbs the layman, but it is a necessary fact of life to the
jumper exhibitor. In actual practice, a drawn-out knock-
down-and-out class, or a series of difficult jump-offs will
drain a lot of strength from even the fittest horse, and
it may be necessary to "coast" with him for a class or
two, or even scratch entirely if he is to have anything
left by the time the Stake or Grand Prix is competed for.
Remember, too, that the smart competitor with two or
three horses to your one will sometimes try to wear
your good horse out in the early classes with his second
string, while keeping his best horse fresh for the later
classes. Also under the category of the more contemplative
form of judgment fall one's reflections on how his horse
has been going during the show and what changes, if any,
one can make in showing him in the next class.

Many of these decisions are difficult ones to make. In
my own case, I try to rely on what I feel to be the
best interests of the horse as a rule of thumb in making
them, and am not, perhaps, as quick to press my horses
as some other exhibitors. It cannot be denied that the
"devil take the hindmost" school of thought, which is
concerned only with immediate implications of a situation
and not tomorrow's class, continues to flourish and to
do, sometimes, much better than I would have expected—
but I've never been able to make it work for me. The
best one can do is to learn to make his own decisions in
these matters, and hope to profit from his own mistakes.

Even more important to the show rider is the kind
of judgment that must become instinctive, or at least
almost instantaneous. For here he must be not a reflective
weigher of alternatives, but a gambler: part odds maker;

part poker player. The rider must learn to calculate, quite accurately, his chances of success in attempting the whole range of difficult things he may be called upon to ask his horse to do in the show ring. As at the race track, only the winning bets pay off; it is what you accomplish that counts, not what you attempt—no matter how correctly—and fail to accomplish.

This seems self-evident, but a surprising number of riders cling to some hazy notion of what is "correct" riding even when they know deep inside that it's not going to work. "Why did you let your horse come so fast at the gate—did you really think he would make it going at that pace?" we may ask. "No, I thought he'd hit it," is often the answer, "but I didn't want to check him." It's very nice to meet all your fences going forward, but it's still not so important as giving your horse a really fair chance to jump the fence. (There may be more virtue in knocking down a fence because you've tried to do something right than because you've done something wrong—but the real virtue lies in not knocking down the fence at all.)

In schooling, if we encounter something the horse won't do, the first step is to try to find out why. But if we enter the show ring with a horse who can't do something, we are better advised to try to avoid having to ask him to do it.

I don't mean to suggest that showing involves dissimulation—far from it. But if the art of schooling really lies in exploring areas of deficiency and correcting them, then certainly the art of making the best of your horse in the show ring lies largely in protecting him from exposing his principal weaknesses, and trying to arrange things so that he spends as much time as possible on his strongest grounds, and as little on his weakest. In practice, this requires an enormous amount of tact, and the rider must be prepared to "finesse" a good many situations that he would not let pass so readily on the schooling grounds.

For example, the high-strung horse will not infrequently have a tendency to pick up speed on the course, to start to "take us" a bit after he has jumped the first few fences. If we start to fight him, or promptly make a series of half-halts as we would at home, the smoothness of the performance will be lost, and in a hunter class any chance of a ribbon will be lost along with it; but if we do nothing at all, he is likely to start to jump badly, or even dangerously. Under these circumstances the good rider will split the difference and attempt to "kid him along," suggesting rather than insisting, "coasting" a little more on the turns, but never admitting—to the horse—that they really feel the need for stronger measures. (Women riders, who lack confidence in their "brute strength" to begin with, often become particularly adept at these arts of persuasion and deception, and I have seen horses just slip kindly along over an outside course in the ladies' class who had been almost running away with their stronger regular riders.)

There is no quick way to develop this kind of judgment; only experience can teach the rider to distinguish between situations which can be successfully "finessed" and those which will require more drastic measures. But even the experienced rider will find it useful, in making plans for the show ring, to contemplate alternative plans at the same time. Nothing seems so futile as the performance of a rider who has decided on one way of riding a course, and when it doesn't work, can think of nothing but to repeat the same error. Sometimes, for example, we expect our horse to be very much in hand, and to "make the extra stride" in the difficult distances on the course—but if he happens instead to be moving very freely, or happens to meet all his fences "long," it is much better to change the riding plan and leave the extra stride out, instead of insisting on following a plan based on what have proved to be false assumptions. With young horses in particular, the first really serious error that obviates any chance of a ribbon should bring an alternative plan into practice, and the rider should finish with a schooling round that will teach the horse something for his next class, instead of blundering along as if nothing had happened. (But be sure you're *really* out of the ribbons. I have seen riders in large jump-offs on time knock down the first fence, and then just coast around the rest of the course, only to find that none of the competitors who followed could come up with a clean round either, and they had blown a chance at a win!)

Bit by bit, as one continues to show, he will learn to recognize which kinds of things his horse does best in the show ring, and which things he has to be careful about. Generally we find that things do not go quite as well in the show ring as we would expect—for every horse or rider who "moves up" under the stimulus of the excitement of competition and the presence of an audience, there will be five who move down, and most often we will have to "overlearn" our skills in practice if we want them to prove reliable under the stresses of competition.

I have already suggested that before each class the rider

should review the level of his performance during the show with hopes that he can eliminate a certain number of errors in every class he competes in. Between shows, the same thing should take place in a broader, more deliberate way. The show should be reviewed by the rider with complete objectivity, and with particular attention to the weaknesses that were exposed under the pressures of showing. These will be the areas to concentrate on before the next show. Perhaps certain experiments have suggested themselves while the show was in progress. Occasionally it may be necessary to try them during the show, but on average, it is wiser to try every new tactic at home to verify its effectiveness before employing it "where it counts."

While nothing can replace the rider's own analysis of his performance, he may also benefit from comments and criticisms of fellow exhibitors and spectators, for they are sometimes very astute and helpful. But in general, the decisions must be the rider's own. The weakest answer as to why one is doing something is "because so-and-so told me to." The advice may be quite correct; but in this case the rider should know why, and accept it as his own. For quite often, unsolicited advice will prove false; in my experience the tendency seems to be for outsiders to praise you too highly for your good performances, and to condemn you too severely for your poor ones. In the same sense, they are likely to be blind to the defects of the horse who is going relatively well and almost equally blind to the virtues of the horse who is not winning.

I would like to emphasize one final point that is significantly more important in the show ring than in schooling: the importance of correct beginnings. Many riders who conclude a show at their peak form somehow seem unable to concentrate enough, in the first class or two, to be able to make a good start. (As my teammate, Frank Chapot, often says, "You can't win them all unless you win the first class.") The rider who is willing to think about the first class in the show as aggressively as he will think later on will always have a considerable advantage, and almost any considerable advantage is worth taking. It seems to me that both in this country and abroad, the winners of the first class and the last class in a show are more likely to come from the small group of better riders than any others, and there is a lesson to be learned in this.

Good beginnings in a general sense are contingent on good beginnings in a much more specific sense. It would be an exaggeration to say that a good beginning is half the battle in riding a good round, but it is certainly extremely important.

I have often been amazed, while judging shows, at the reliability with which one can anticipate what kind of round the horse is likely to have from his first few steps in the show ring. So many riders never seem to get organized until about halfway round, and start their round with reins too long, a horse with no impulsion, and a crooked line to the first fence. One may not be able to think quickly enough, or improvise brilliantly enough to avoid difficulties in the middle or at the end of a round, but if a rider will concentrate sufficiently, he can certainly start his round well.

To the extent that bad beginnings are sometimes created not by carelessness but by impatience, excitement, or nerves, these are things the rider must learn to control himself. I am told that I appear rather cold and calculating in the ring, though I think of myself as a basically emotional and very high-strung person. I have found that the best way for me to deal with this is to pace myself by becoming quite consciously more deliberate as the tension rises. (For this reason, I have always suspected that the most deliberate pitchers in baseball and tournament players in golf are probably also contradictory in the same sense, and far from being phlegmatic, are likely to be rather high-strung competitors who have learned to channel their nervous energies.)

In this connection, it has often been stated that a horse can always "tell" when a rider is nervous. In the sense that nervous people do nervous things and are likely to betray their anxiety with the smallest gesture, this is usually true in practice. But I doubt very much that it *needs* to be true. It is quite possible to divorce one's actions quite completely from one's frame of mind, and to relax almost mechanically even in the most anxiety-fraught situation. It has often been noted that the very inexperienced rider (or the rider who is not very bright) will sometimes ride the bad horse amazingly well by riding him "as if he were a good horse." I have often verified in my own experience that the same results can be achieved without shutting off your brain by learning to divorce sufficiently your overt actions from your mental attitude. In other words, it is quite possible to have a low estimate of a horse's ability, or to be extremely apprehensive about the level of performance one will achieve; and yet if you ride confidently and well, and ask confidently and soundly for the horse's best level of performance, his response will be to the ride you give him, and not to your secret thoughts. It is true that horses are extremely sensitive physically; but their "sixth sense" and "their mind-reading ability" are, it seems to me, functions of this physical sensitivity and not intuitions of a higher order. We may well be grateful for this, for it enables our horses to extricate us sometimes from "impossible" situations, and carry us serenely over fences we "know" they can't jump!

Riding F. E. I. Classes

Jumping competitions conducted under the rules of the Fédération Equestre Internationale (F.E.I.) fall into two principal categories: classes in which time is the determining factor in the event of equality of faults, and classes in which time is no factor (except for exceeding the time allowed). When most American exhibitors think of F.E.I. classes they tend to think only of the first category, and I think it's fair to say that, as a group, they don't think very lovingly of it. Speed classes, they argue, make the rider run his horse off his feet and spoil his temperament, and sadly, they are often right in practice—not because this weakness is implicit in speed classes as such, but because so many speed classes are competed over courses which are not really suitable.

For properly, the course should place just as much premium on the ability to go the shortest distance as it does on the ability to jump at a faster pace, and the description *Epreuve de maniabilité*—"test of handiness"—

is used interchangeably in Europe with *Zeitspringen*, or "time jumping." Far more time classes are won on the strength of the horse's ability to turn and to jump fences at difficult angles than on the ability to "run and jump" by itself, and these two abilities tend to exclude each other very often. (It is rarely a good idea to "leave out a stride" at the fence that precedes a sharp turn, for the length of stride required to make the long stand-back will usually ruin the turn that follows.)

When the course designer has afforded sufficient opportunities to save time by turning or "playing angles," the main complaint against speed competitions is invalidated, and their very important advantage becomes evident: they afford the average good jumper with classes he has a chance to win on the basis of his state of training as well as his ability, against horses who can jump a bigger fence. In Europe there are always half a dozen or more horses in competition who have the capacity to jump 7 feet or higher—and how is one to beat them with just the "good" jumper whose limit is, say 5 feet 6 inches, if the only form of class requires successive jump-offs? I love the jump-off classes, too, and my pulse quickens like anyone else's as the fences get higher and higher, but for me horse shows lose a great deal when they leave no place for the average good horse, just as golf tournaments would lose most of their appeal if they deteriorated into driving contests that were concerned only with the golfer's "length from the tee."

Laymen (and some riders, too) are often surprised by the actual time on the clock of different kinds of rounds, for the horse who is cleverly ridden at a smooth and even pace, making very economical turns and only very rarely checking, never *seems* as fast as the horse that is racing wildly around. But the observer who really knows where fast times come from will know that the horse who is almost running away can hardly stay within ten seconds of the obedient horse over the average course. Loose turns and excessive checking are the two commonest ways of wasting time on the course, and the horse's actual "turn of speed" rarely has very much to do with the result.

One simple rule that sums up many of the factors that make for fast times in speed competitions is simply "Always go right to the next fence." Riders who gained most of their experience under AHSA rules under which time was not a factor usually find this difficult to do, for they are accustomed to jumping a fence, pulling up and getting reorganized, and then looking for the next one. The better practice, however, is to jump a fence and go to the next one on the most direct line possible; and *when you get there*, reorganize or check if necessary.

When time is precious, don't waste it by checking the horse's speed a dozen strides from the next fence, or making careless turns, for these expenditures of time provide little assurance that you will jump the fence any better when you *do* get to it. But when time is not a factor, as in Puissance classes, use it liberally, and take all the room you need to make the best approach you can to the next fence. Puissance classes exist for the "super horses" who can jump enormous fences, and many truly great horses lack the brute strength that is required to win one in first-class company, and never enter them. (I don't recall ever having seen Merano, for example, entered in a regular Puissance.)

Generally speaking, the rider's approach to very big

Puissance fences will be exactly the same in kind as his approach to smaller obstacles, except that he will find it less possible to jump them as an extension of the horse's normal stride. Inexperienced riders usually think that it takes a lot of pace to jump very big fences, and they are quite wrong; not much pace is necessary if you can get to the right take-off spot with sufficient impulsion. The best Puissance and high-jump riders rarely use more than three or four driving strides before the take-off, but they develop excellent accuracy in finding the best take-off distance and always maintain impulsion while they are looking for it.

There is some difference of opinion regarding the ideal take-off for a very high fence. Normally, of course, we look for a take-off point that is a foot or so farther from the fence than the height of the fence itself, and try to stand back 5 to 6 feet from the base of a 4-foot vertical fence. But in my opinion, few horses can jump the *very* high fence—say, over 6 feet—from a stand-back that is an extension of the driving stride, and when fences reach that height I begin to look for a take-off from a very strong, shorter, "hock-gathering" stride that would be just about the height of the fence away. (Ksar d'Esprit has taken me over 7 feet or better on almost half a dozen occasions now, and his successful attempts have all been made from about 7 feet from the base of the fence, not 8 or 9 feet.) This shorter stride must never be so short that it robs the horse of impulsion, but a 7-foot wall is not a good fence to be "reaching for " either!

CHAPTER 10

Analyzing Courses

Analyzing Courses

Considering the number of factors that go into the performance of a clear round over a difficult jumping course, and the number of right decisions that have to be made and executed, each in its particular way, the task seems overwhelmingly difficult. I used to think that the best riders (and the best performers in other complex activities as well) were those who had somehow learned to think of everything at once, and I often despaired of ever duplicating this accomplishment.

Through the years, however, I have come to believe that almost the opposite situation is closer to the truth. Precisely because the horse's and rider's mechanisms and their interrelationship are so complex, it now seems to me that the most successful riders are those who have learned how to *simplify* their problems most effectively.

One way of doing this, as I have already indicated, is by forging a basic riding technique at home that is solid enough to permit one to concentrate more on ends than on means while he is in the show ring; another is by analyzing and anticipating the difficulties the course will present, and clarifying as many as possible of those difficult decisions in advance.

Some of my show-ring friends have accused me of making the business of jumping a series of fences too complicated by thinking about strides and distances, but as I've said, I believe it's just the other way round—analyzing courses and "figuring distances" is a means of simplifying something that is in fact very complex. For whether we appraise the course from outside the ring or on foot inside it, we will simplify the problems it presents if we can understand their nature more accurately. (I am always happiest when I can walk the course on foot before I ride it, as riders are invariably permitted to do in Europe; but failing this opportunity, all the essentials can be deduced from watching a few rounds over the course from outside the ring.)

The basic components of the jumper course, as I mentioned briefly in the previous chapter, are simply the isolated fence, the fences in various long but related distances, and all the different varieties of the combination. If we can verify on foot, or learn from watching other horses how each of the fences on the course is likely to "meet" the average horse, we can free our minds from the necessity of making quite a large number of unnecessary decisions. Let me illustrate what I mean.

A typical hunter or jumper course in the ring might consist of a brush, a gate, a stone wall, and an in-and-out of rails, this circuit to be jumped twice. If we can measure or deduce the distances, and understand our horse, this means that we will really only need to depend on our "eye" and our judgment of distance four times in order to negotiate the ten fences. We will, of course, have to find our own distance at the first and the third fence both times around; but the way we meet the second fence and the in-and-out on each occasion will be largely determined by the way the horse negotiates the fences preceding them and the distances involved. The same thing will be true of a longer, more complex course; out of eighteen fences, the rider may have eight or ten decisions regarding take-off that will depend on his judgment entirely, and eight or ten that are already partially determined for him.

The factors involved in these decisions consist primarily of the length of the horse's stride at various rates of speed, and the length of the arc he will make at those speeds in jumping fences of various types and dimensions. D'Endrödy's book contains a valuable tabulation of these measurements and a formula for utilizing them in solving distance problems. His measurements are actual ones, and a close study of them will save the rider a good deal of time in jumping on sandy ground where the actual footfall can be observed and measured. Nonetheless, it will be to every rider's advantage to verify d'Endrödy's observations for himself, at least to the extent of watching where horses actually take off and land over various types of fences, and noting how long a stride they are able to take at various speeds, for this is the only way to develop facility in measuring with the eye where one is likely to land, and what kind of take-off he is likely to be able to make under various conditions.

D'Endrödy's approach to the problem of distance is a fastidious one, and his solution can be worked out on paper. However, while his calculations express the actual basis of the rule-of-thumb methods most of us apply in practice, we are often compelled by lack of time (or lack of a mind for figures) to employ a less meticulous but quicker method of solving the same problems.

The first essential in analyzing courses is knowing one's own horse's stride, and what can be done with it. The rider must know, in terms of feeling as well as mathematics, where his horse's stride falls in relation to the stride of other horses, and how much he can lengthen or shorten it. The application of this knowledge is very simple.

If I watch three or four horses negotiate the course ahead of me, and they take about the same length of normal stride as my horse, I can work out in my mind exactly what I must do by observing what happens to them. In other words, let us suppose that the first horse jumps the first fence, takes six normal strides, and gets a bit "under" the second fence, making a "proppy" jump. Immediately I know that if I jump the first fence normally and at a similar pace, I will have a choice of either taking back slightly, and jumping the second fence after six slightly shortened strides, or landing over the first fence and moving on, and then being able to stand back and jump the second fence in five strides. In either case, the second fence is likely to be a good deal smoother than it would be if I had to wait until I saw the distance myself to determine what I should do; by observing another horse or two over the course, we gain in advance the knowledge of what we will have to do instantly upon landing.

When a choice exists, the decision of which alternative to

take will depend largely on the particular horse one is riding and his particular talents. In the case above, if the horse had a good ability to "stand back" at his fences and no temperamental problems that might be magnified by slipping along a bit, one would probably use the five-stride alternative, which would probably make for a smoother performance. On the other hand, if the horse were not particularly courageous, or had a tendency to hurry if "asked" very much, one would be more likely (particularly early on the course) to proceed very quietly and take the extra stride.

The process is even simpler when one is permitted to walk the distances on foot. The rider must first learn how much he must extend his own normal walking stride in order to take 36-inch steps, for the most convenient norm to use in figuring distances is the twelve-foot stride at 350 yards per minute. (Thus four of the rider's strides will equal one of his horse's.) It is helpful at first to verify this with a tape measure, but as long as the rider can maintain reasonable accuracy, he can disregard the actual mathematical distance and proceed by feel, lengthening his own stride or shortening it as circumstances may dictate.

In approaching any fence, the rider must be conscious of the line to the fence that follows (so that he can take it into account in selecting the line to the fence at hand); he must note any details of appearance that might tend to startle his horse when he comes later to jump his round, and any peculiarities of structure that might tend to make a knock-down less likely by jumping one side of the fence in preference to the other. (Needless to say, with a basically safe jumper the rider always tries to jump the strongest part of the fence.) It is also occasionally necessary to think of the position of the sun when considering the line of approach to the fence, for late in the afternoon it may be necessary to angle some fence on the course to avoid being blinded by heading directly toward the sun on the horizon.

After walking the chosen line to the first fence, the rider picks out with his eye the place on the far side that he judges will be the normal landing area for a horse who has jumped the fence normally at the pace at which he plans to ride the course, and proceeds to the next fence in strides based on that pace. Let us assume that he is going to ride this course at about 350 yards per minute, and that he is keeping track of the strides by counting to himself "ONE, two, three, four; TWO, two, three, four," and so forth. If he arrives at a reasonable take-off point for the next fence on a "four"—implying the completion of a normal stride—then he knows that he may ride the first two fences completely normally, and that if he succeeds in finding a good take-off for the first fence, he will almost surely meet the second fence "in stride."

On the other hand, when the rider arrives at what he judges to be an appropriate take-off spot on an *uncompleted* stride, the situation becomes slightly more complicated. If he is only one step out, he would normally ride the distance in the closest full stride. (That is to say, if the correct take-off point falls at the third step in stride number four, he would ride the whole distance a bit more steadily, and make four shorter strides; if on the other hand, the correct distance should fall on the first step of his fifth stride, he would ride a bit more freely, and ride the distance as four long strides.

Needless to say, the most difficult case is the distance that is exactly a half-stride out. Let's say that, walking normally, the rider finds the distance to be four strides plus two steps. His decision to ride in four strides or in five will be dictated partly by the particular abilities of the horse he is riding and partly by the particular type of class and the particular type of fences involved. If both fences are spread fences, or if the class is a class in which time will be the determining factor, he is almost obliged to ride for the long stride, and overcome the unevenness of the distance by omitting the extra half-stride. If, on the other hand, he is riding a horse who lacks courage, a horse who tends to flatten out when he "stands back," or a horse whose tendency is to pick up speed on the course, or if the second fence is a vertical one, he would more often attempt the first fence rather carefully, and take five short strides to the second fence.

When a turn will follow the next fence instead of another fence in the same line, the rider should still walk the turn, and in speed classes the selection of turning points will be just as important as knowing the distances between the related fences on the course. (When time is invoked only on the first or second jump-off, the rider must be sure to note whether or not the course for the jump-off is shortened, for if, as usual, it is, he must remember to walk his turns for the jump-off course as well; many a class has been won by riders who noticed a possibility of turning inside one of the omitted fences when jumping the shortened course.)

The distances in combinations are walked in the same manner as the longer distances, but the rider may have to walk them two or three times, using strides of different lengths and altering his take-off and landing points, before he finds a solution that seems feasible. The 28-foot to

31-foot distance, which may be either one *very* long stride, or two *very* short ones, is almost always a hard decision to make—but the trend of courses in Europe at the major shows is to demand of riders more and more of these "odd distance" decisions. This type of problem assumes its most difficult form in the combination that requires an alternation of very long and very short strides, and in the combination that requires the horse and rider to attempt one or more of the component fences in what is normally the most difficult way in order to make a solution of the whole problem possible.

As a typical example of what I mean, the combination 12 a, b, c, from Count Leuwenhaupt's brilliantly conceived course for the Stockholm Olympic Games in 1956 posed the following problem for horse and rider: The first fence of the combination was a big oxer, spread some 7 feet, which one met exactly on a half-stride from the preceding fence. The second fence, two short strides away, was a vertical white gate at the maximum height of 5 feet 3 inches. The third element was another large oxer, one *very* long stride away from the gate (as I recall, the distance was 28 feet to the near rail of an oxer spread about two meters). In this case, if the rider elected to leave out the half-stride so as to meet the first oxer very boldly, the two short strides that had to follow became very, very difficult. Yet if he chose instead to make the extra stride approaching the combination, and to jump the oxer off a short stride in order to facilitate the negotiation of the short distance that followed, he ran a considerably larger risk of incurring a fault at the very first fence of a big combination, thus increasing the likelihood of additional faults in the form of either knock-downs or refusals at the remaining two fences. Both solutions were difficult, and had to be executed very skillfully to become possible.

In this particular case, I think that more of the horses who met the combination on a short stride got through it without fault, though as I recall, Halla, the Gold Medal winner, jumped the first oxer off a long stride in the morning and off a short stride in the afternoon and was clean both times. My own horse, Night Owl, didn't steady very willingly after jumping the water (No. 10, the first fence on the line that ended over the combination), and so I elected to gamble in the morning round and stand back at the first oxer, knowing that he'd at least get over *that*. He did, but landed in so deep that he hit the vertical fence hard, and, off balance, hit the last oxer as well, to my sorrow! In the afternoon I insisted on the extra stride coming to the combination, and got through it without fault.

General Lombardi's courses for the 1960 Olympic Games posed more problems of the same kind, though, in characteristically Roman fashion, the difficulties were less apparent when walking the course than when riding it. The heart of the Piazza di Siena Course for the Individual Medal was a three-combination consisting of a red wall, a triple bar over brush, and a square oxer. The first distance was one long stride (about 25 feet to the near rail of a 6-foot spread); the second was about 30 feet to the near rail of the oxer, which would be one almost impossibly long stride, or two *extremely* short ones. Winkler and Halla (who can pick up impulsion with almost incredible speed) jumped it as one stride, one stride, but the only solution with the average very good horse was one stride, two. Ideally, one would like to approach the stone wall

quite steadily, and *plan* to reach for the triple bar as much
as one dared, in order to land as close to the far rail as
possible, and leave a bit more room for the two strides
before the oxer. This was the tactic successfully employed
by Raimondo d'Inzeo and Posilippo, but it would be a
risky one, of course, with a horse who might have an inclination to stop or who was not very careful behind. As it
was, only a handful of horses jumped this combination
clean twice, and sixty of the ninety-seven performances
over it incurred some penalty.

The course for the Prize of Nations in Rome's Olympic
Stadium (see diagram) also tended to concentrate its
difficulties in its combinations. The two-combination (No.
10), a pair of big, perfectly parallel oxers with a 24-foot
inside measurement, was difficult primarily because it was
so big and so square, and because one met it coming off
a sharp turn, with only four or five strides in which to
"arrange something." In such cases, one is usually wise to
avoid getting too deep into the corner, and to try to maintain a fair amount of impulsion even while making the
turn; in the second round, when Ksar jumped it clean for
me after a fault the first time, I let him shade the corner
a little more, and I wish I'd done it in the morning as
well.

The three-combination (No. 5) in the course for the
team class at Rome was an easier variation of the combination we had jumped in the individual class. This time
the triple bar was the first fence, 24 feet from the wall,
which was now a longish two strides (36 feet) from the
first element of another rather square oxer. Again the triple
bar was the key to jumping the combination, but this time
the safest course lay in the opposite tactic, and insuring

that the horse would *not* have to reach for the triple bar; for while a "stand-back" at the triple bar meant only a little reach for the wall, the two strides to the oxer became quite uncomfortably long. Fortunately, the close take-off at the triple bar was quite easy to arrange, for the No. 5 combination was just six and a half strides from fence No. 4, some perfectly straightforward planks, and the rider had only to choose the option of making seven strides between them to arrive very nicely at the combination. In most cases those riders who approached the combination in seven steady strides with good impulsion experienced no difficulty, while most of the refusals and faults were made by horses who simply "kept coming" blindly in six strides, and found no good move to make by the time they had jumped the wall. It is exactly in such situations as this that the rider who can analyze the course accurately can relieve himself of the necessity of *outriding* his opponent by *outthinking* him, and while this may give him an edge only once or twice on the course, the advantage gained may well make the difference between a ribbon and simply another entry fee gone down the drain.

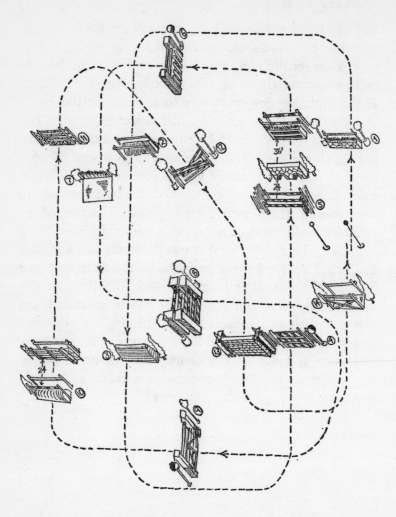

COURSE FOR THE GRAND PRIX DES NATIONS, XVII OLYMPIC
GAMES, ROME, 1960
(Course diagram courtesy H. Stewart Treviranus)

CHAPTER 11

Learning from Observation

Learning from Observation

In dedicating this book to my teachers I had in mind a much larger group than the handful of hardy souls who tried to pass on to me the elements of riding skill in periods of more or less formal instruction. Sound teaching will very much accelerate the rider's development by focusing on his own particular weaknesses, and will save him a great deal of time that might otherwise be spent in persevering or experimenting along fruitless lines, and I will always be grateful to Ada Thompson, Gordon Wright, Frank Carroll, "Cappy" Smith, and our team coach, Bertalan de Nemethy, for the very important part they have played in helping me to attain my own riding objectives. But the rider's education must be a process of active learning as well as active teaching, and if we regard our teachers as all those from whom we can learn something, their number becomes legion; in this sense all that we require in order to become pupils of the world's great riders is an open and inquiring mind and an objective eye.

The teaching and learning of riding is not quite so easy as it sounds, I'm afraid. Many good riders, and even some people who are considered good teachers, are limited in their ability to evaluate accurately another rider's performance because they have lost the capacity to really see what is there; instead, they see only what they want to see. So it is a common experience to find a performance praised because some detail of it that is particularly important to the observer has been performed in accordance with the dogma he espouses—and it is most common of all to find that the level of success achieved in terms of placing in the show ring has prejudiced the observer so that he no longer properly weighs the ingredients with which the success was achieved.

I have already mentioned that in my own case I have often been praised for a poorly ridden performance which happened, under the particular circumstances, to be a winning one; and I have also been roundly and generally criticized for performances in which I felt I had given something approaching my best because, under the circumstances, they were *not* winning ones. Human nature being what it is, we must become accustomed to being praised too generously for a win, and criticized too severely when we lose—but we must never lose our own perspective, or accept uncritically either the abuse or, especially, the praise.

Not only in his own riding, but in watching the efforts of others, the rider will learn much of value if an unbiased eye tells him what is going on, and an open mind searches out the why's and how's. "What am I doing that makes the horses I ride pull more than so-and-so's horses?" "How does that rider manage to keep his horses so much better balanced on their turns than mine?" "What is that famous rider trying to accomplish by working his horse in that way?" These are the kinds of questions we must ask ourselves continually, and we must continue to re-evaluate our own experience and our own observations even when we are quite sure that we know the right answers.

Many riders, myself included, find it helpful to keep a notebook of tentative answers to questions such as these in a kind of personal shorthand. Last year's "discoveries" often make amusing reading today, when the imperfections of our "old" thinking are so clear, but even this reflects some kind of progress, and a review of the random observations of a year will often reveal quite clearly the general areas of experimentation that seem to have produced the most fruitful results. "Ksar is beating you by throwing away a leg that is rigid rather than clinging—don't let him make you ride like X," I might remind myself, referring to a rider who neglects to maintain the liveliness of his horses' hind legs, and ends up trying to do all his riding with his hands. "Watch the very long rein—are you bringing hands back to the mouth instead of moving horse up to the bit? Cf. St. Cyr." So might read a warning to apply to tomorrow's work, after a day when one's horses hadn't gone very well. Perhaps it will not prove to have been the thing that was being neglected today, but at least it will provide a starting point for tomorrow's thinking, and some hope that tomorrow's deficiencies will not merely duplicate today's.

The fact that our ideas about riding seem to be in a

constant state of evolution probably accounts for the fact that few writers on the subject seem to be able to read their words in print without wanting to start immediately a new book of amplifications, corrections, and additions. There are few ideas in the present work that have not survived the test of practice for a period of several years; but in all honesty, my experience tells me that before long I will begin to find things I'd like to change.

It is never wise to be too hasty in your judgment, or too certain that you have all the right answers. "Life is short, art is long"—and the fact that you know *something* by no means implies that you know *everything*. Even among "experts" it is rare to find two people who see exactly the same thing in a given performance, or interpret what they see in exactly the same way. The people who have impressed me as being the best judges of performance are characterized by their objectivity in weighing apparently contradictory evidence. Hans Winkler, for example, is as quick to acknowledge a virtue in a rider or horse he had previously disparaged, or to re-explore a despised theory on the basis of evidence that it can produce desirable results under *some* set of circumstances, as he is to state his own position; and he looks at everything, and not only the things that he would prefer to see.

One may be tempted to say that it would be simpler and more pleasant if riding were the kind of activity that required no constant re-examination and re-evaluation of one's theories and practices, but of course just the opposite is true—riding makes a sport for a lifetime because its range *is* so great, and a lifetime is such a short span in which to explore it.

The best teacher of all, if you examine his instructions

carefully enough, is no writer, no instructor, no other rider—it is the horse you are riding, and his performance will always be the soundest criterion of all of the appropriateness and "correctness" of your actions. Because it is his movement that is the most important thing, the role of the photograph as an aid to criticizing riders' techniques is often misunderstood—for the static moment that is preserved on film is, in a sense, a moment that never existed; riding is a continuum rather than a succession of static moments.

Thus, while there is no one supremely correct position but only a range of positions that are correct in relation to the corresponding movement and balance of the horse, we are often shown "classic" pictures in which certain details of position are "according to the book"—heels down, a straight line from the rider's elbow to the bit—and yet in which the "feeling" is wrong. By "feeling" in this case I mean the relationship between the rider's balance and the horse's, insofar as their joint continuum of movement can be reconstructed from the moment at which the picture was snapped.

I can think of one widely reproduced picture in particular which has often been praised as a good example of "correct position"; the rider's hand and leg positions at the moment the shutter opened indeed appear orthodox, but the position of the horse suggests that the movement must have been quite wrong. I can never look at this picture without concluding that the horse's extension reflects too long a take-off, and that the rider has failed to compensate for this extraordinary effort and is, in fact coming back. I would be very surprised if a picture of the same jump taken a split-second later wouldn't show the rider already well behind the horse, and the horse hitting the fence behind.

Just as some bad jumps can make "good" pictures, so is the opposite true. How many riders love to pick faults in photographs of the most famous show jumpers, castigating this detail of position or that, without ever recognizing the most important thing the picture shows, a harmony of balance and movement.

The illustrations contained in this book were chosen primarily for their justness of "feeling," and I hope the reader will be able to discern the important lessons they have to teach about this. The particular details of position vary somewhat, for these are riders using position as a means and not as an end; they show riders trying to win important competitions, not riders demonstrating a seat. Moreover, they show riders who have won the most important competitions—Olympic Gold Medals, World Championships, and Grands Prix. Criticize their personal idiosyncracies if you will, but study the things they have in common very carefully; what you are looking at are the common denominators of success!

To the reader who has borne with me to the end of this collection of observations on riding and jumping, my thanks for his kind attention. To those wiser and perhaps grayer heads that have long since become aware of the imperfections of the present work, my apologies and my respect; and to those younger riders who may, I hope, have found something of value in the preceding pages—a new idea, or a new approach—my best wishes for their future success.

c